Tell Me About
History

Tell Me About
History

WATERBIRD BOOKS
Columbus, Ohio

This edition published in the United States of America in 2004 by
Waterbird Books
an imprint of McGraw-Hill Children's Publishing,
a Division of The McGraw-Hill Companies
8720 Orion Place
Columbus, Ohio 43240-2111

www.MHkids.com

Library of Congress Cataloging-in-Publication Data is on file with the publisher.

Printed in China

ISBN 0-7696-3381-1

1 2 3 4 5 6 7 8 9 10 TOP 09 08 07 06 05 04

Contents

WHO?

CONTENTS

WHO WERE THE FRANKS?

Frankish soldiers

The Franks emerged from the ruins of the Roman Empire in 476 A.D. as the dominant people of western Europe. Their leader, Clovis, enlarged his lands around the Rhine River in Germany through war. By 540 A.D. the Franks ruled most of the old Roman province of Gaul, France, named after the Franks.

The first Frankish ruling family was the Merovingian dynasty, named after Clovis's grandfather, Meroveus. Clovis became a Christian. He made Paris his capital city. Most of the Franks were peasant farmers, who lived on lands ruled by nobles. The peasants raised food, performing the seasonal tasks of ploughing, sowing, and harvesting. They also had to fight for their lord when he went to war. The Frankish system of land-holding and service was the beginning of the feudal system in Europe.

Charlemagne was king of the Franks from 768 to 814, and created a vast empire. On Christmas Day 800, the pope crowned Charlemagne Holy Roman Emperor. After the rule of Charlemagne, the Frankish empire began to break apart.

FACT FILE

The Frankish king Charlemagne introduced this writing, called *Carolingian script*, which was easier for people to read and write.

WHO WERE THE HITTITES?

Hittite charioteers

The Hittites arrived in what is now Anatolia, in Turkey, from either central Europe or central Asia in about 2000 B.C. During the next 500 years, they expanded their territory to parts of Syria in the south and Mesopotamia in the east. Like the Sumerians and Egyptians, they could gather large armies, and were among the first people to use chariots in war. Archers fired arrows from the chariots, giving them an edge over their enemies.

One of the first battles for which accounts remain occurred in 1282 B.C. at Kadesh, on the Orontes River. Mutwatallis, the Hittite leader, fought a battle against Egyptian forces under Rameses II. The Hittites were winning, but Rameses managed to regroup when the Hittites stopped fighting to loot Egyptian equipment. Both sides claimed it as a victory, but it was inconclusive, and the two sides signed a non-aggression treaty.

FACT FILE

The Hittites were the first to master iron-making. This can be seen in their weaponry. Axe heads were made from bronze, as shown here, and also iron.

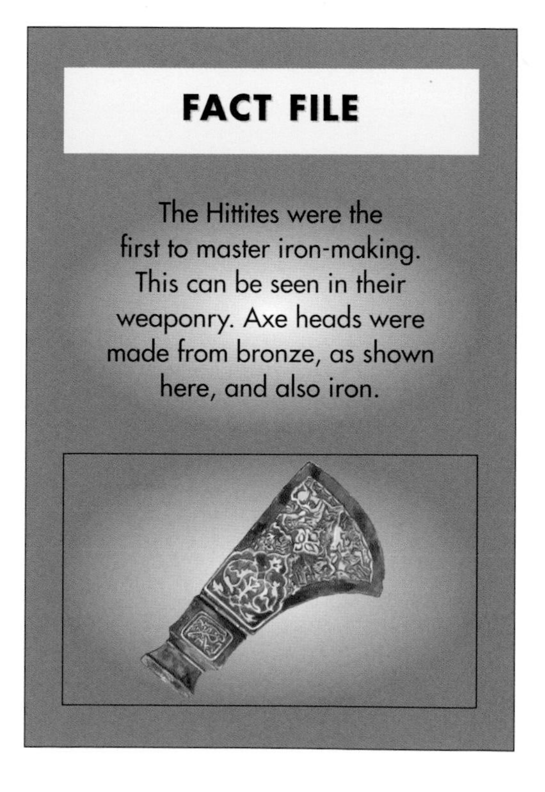

WHO WERE THE OLMECS AND CHAVINS?

Two groups developed America's earliest civilizations, in Mexico and Central America, and in Peru on the west coast of South America.

The Olmecs flourished between about 1200 and 400 B.C. They made pottery and cleared the jungle to grow crops. The Olmec people constructed large stepped pyramids from earth. They also held religious ceremonies and worshipped their gods in temples built on top of these pyramids.

The Olmecs

The Chavins were people living in the Andes foothills, who became farmers by about 1000 B.C. They built the first towns in South America. They cut terraces into hillsides and became expert at irrigation to cultivate the dry land and mountain slopes.

FACT FILE

In modern Peru, craftworkers carry on the traditions of their Chavin ancestors, producing bright, handwoven textiles. Designs like these have been produced in Peru for 3,000 years.

The Chavins

WHO DID THE PERSIANS WORSHIP?

The people of ancient Persia believed in nature gods, such as the sun and the sky. Many of their gods were adaptations of Indian gods, such as Mithra, the god of light, and Varuna, Nasatyas, and Indra. The picture to the right shows a man killing a bull as a sacrifice to renew his life.

Many people followed the teachings of the prophet Zoroaster (or Zarathustra), *c.* 628 to 551 B.C., who reformed the ancient religion. He taught that life was a struggle between good (light) and evil (darkness). He preached a faith based on good thoughts, words, and deeds, emphasising the importance of the god Ahura Mazda, "the wise spirit." This god had become the supreme god because he was the royal family's personal protector. Zoroaster's followers gradually spread his religion through Persia as well as parts of Greece and India.

FACT FILE

Darius I ruled Persia from 521 to 486 B.C. He encouraged trade through the use of coins and new canals. Darius sent an army into Greece in 490 B.C., but Athenian forces defeated it at Marathon. Darius died in 486 B.C. while preparing for new attacks on Greece.

WHO WAS ASOKA?

Asoka

Asoka was the third emperor of the Mauryan dynasty, who ruled the first empire to unite almost all of India. The empire was founded by Asoka's grandfather, Chandragupta Maurya, in about 324 B.C., when he seized the throne of Magadha, a rich kingdom in the Ganges Valley. His son and grandson, Asoka, continued to expand the empire. At its height, it ruled most of India and a large part of Afghanistan.

Ashoka eventually became sickened by the slaughter, and he turned to the pacifist religion of Buddhism. He became one of its greatest supporters, and sent missionaries to his neighbors. He then set out to reform his empire by instigating a new taxation system, and building new cities and roads to promote trade and agriculture in the villages. Asoka made new laws and had them inscribed on stone pillars set up all across his empire. The empire broke up after his death. The last emperor died in 185 B.C.

FACT FILE

The carved stone lions on the pillar at Sarnath have become a national emblem for India.

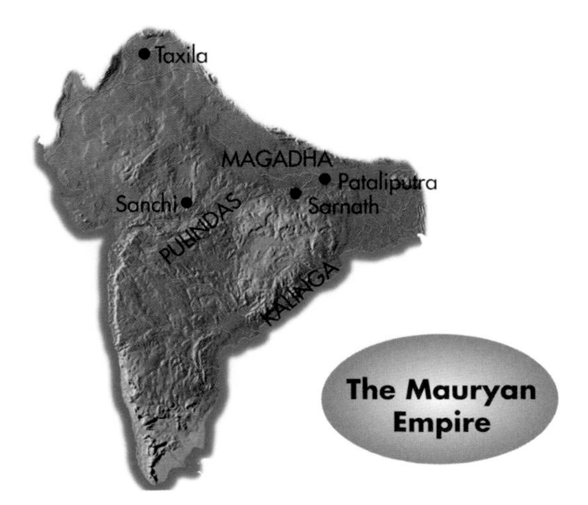

The Mauryan Empire

WHO WAS THE "MAID OF ORLEANS"?

During the Hundred Years War (1337 to 1453), English kings often claimed the throne of France. In 1420, Henry V had forced the French king, Charles VI, to declare him heir to the French throne, rather than his own son, Charles VII. The English controlled all of northern France, but southern France denied the English claim.

Jeanne d'Arc, as she is known in France, was born in 1412 at Domrémy, near Nancy. She was a devout Catholic and, by the age of 13, was having visions telling her that she had been chosen by God to help King Charles VII drive out the English. In 1429, she persuaded the king, and in April of that year she led French troops to lift the seige of Orleans. A series of further wins took the French army to Reims, where all French coronations took place. There, Charles was crowned in July.

Joan was captured in May 1430 by the Burgundian army, who sold her to the English. They burned her at the stake as a heretic at the end of May 1431. She is still revered today as a national heroine in France.

FACT FILE

Medieval castles and towns were fortified to give citizens protection. Sieges could last for months. If attackers could not batter their way into a town, they would try to prevent any supplies of food or armaments reaching the defenders, forcing them to give up or starve.

WHO DID THE ANCIENT GREEKS WORSHIP?

The Greeks believed in many different gods. Chief among these was a family of supernatural beings who lived on Mount Olympus and watched over humanity. Certain gods looked after the harvest; others cared for wild animals, the sea, war, and the like. The king of the gods was Zeus, whom the Romans called Jupiter. The first Olympic Games, which took place in 776 B.C., were held in his honor.

Zeus

Greeks believed that the universe was a sphere. The upper half was light and airy, the lower half dark and gloomy, and the earth was a flat disc, floating between these two halves. When people died, they went to the Underworld, which was ruled by Hades, the brother of Zeus. Poseidon was the Greek god of the sea, often shown carrying a three-pronged spear, called a trident. The Greeks believed Poseidon to be the brother of Zeus and Hades. Poseidon was also associated with earthquakes and horses. The Greeks thought that he was the father of the winged horse, Pegasus.

Poseidon

FACT FILE

The ruins of Greek and Roman temples can be seen across Europe, the Near East, and North Africa. Every town had its own temple, which was dedicated to a protector god or goddess.

WHO WAS ALFRED THE GREAT?

In the late ninth century, most of the northeastern half of England was under the control of the Danish Vikings. The West Saxons had been at war with them for years when Alfred the Great (849 to 899) came to the throne in 871. After years of war, Alfred reconquered London in 886, made peace with the Vikings, and began the process of uniting the kingdoms of England under his leadership.

With more resources at his disposal, Alfred could fortify strategic points and protect the coast with a large fleet.

Alfred was an effective peacetime ruler. Parts of his code of laws are still recognizable in the English legal system. He also encouraged learning and literature, including the translation of Christian texts into Old English to promote a cultural revival in England.

FACT FILE

The Alfred jewel was found near Athelney, in Somerset in 1693. It may be part of a bookmark. On it are the words "Alfred had me made" in Latin.

WHO WAS THE FIRST NORMAN KING OF ENGLAND?

The first Norman king of England was William I, the Conqueror (1027 to 1087). He was born around 1027 in Falaise, in Normandy, the son of Duke Robert I. He became duke upon his father's death in 1035.

In 1066, after the death of Edward the Confessor, William claimed the English throne had been granted to him by Edward. When Edward's brother-in-law, Harold, was elected to the throne by the English nobles, William had no choice but to invade. William's army won the battle known as the Battle of Hastings on October 14.

William was crowned in Westminster Abbey on Christmas Day. From the start, he ruled with an iron fist, taking lands from the Saxons. In 1086, he commissioned the great survey of every property in the country, the Domesday Survey. He started what became known as the feudal system. In return for grants of land, his followers had to swear allegiance and supply men for military service. Their followers had to do likewise, down the social scale to the serfs (slaves).

FACT FILE

At the Battle of Hastings, the English, who fought on foot, resisted as Norman cavalry charged their shield wall and fired arrows at them. When the Normans pretended retreat, the English chased them downhill and were slaughtered. This is recorded in 72 scenes on the famous Bayeux Tapestry.

WHO WERE THE TEUTONIC KNIGHTS?

In the middle ages, various religious orders of knights were formed to serve on the crusades to the Holy Land, to reclaim it for Christianity. The word *crusade* is derived from the Latin, *crux*, meaning "cross." Not only knights went crusading but everyone from kings down.

One such twelfth-century order of crusaders was the Teutonic Knights, German crusaders. They based their organization on two earlier militant orders, the Knights Templars and the Knights Hospitalers.

Once their role in the crusades was over, in the thirteenth century, the Teutonic Knights fought in central and eastern Europe, where they acquired vast territories and attempted to convert pagans in the lands around the Baltic. Like many orders, their influence was a threat to those in power. For example, the Knights Templar had earlier been declared illegal in many countries. This did not happen to the Teutonic Knights, but their power was reduced and they eventually disbanded.

FACT FILE

At the end of the crusades, many of the knights stayed on to guard the conquered land. They were known to build fine castles.

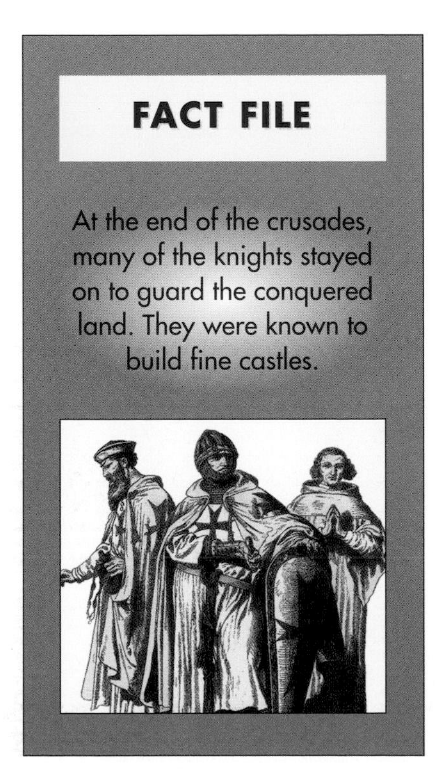

WHO WAS DON QUIXOTE?

FACT FILE

Until the mid-1800s, when pens with steel points became popular, most people wrote with quill pens. The feather was trimmed to a point with a knife.

Don Quixote is a novel written in two parts (1605 and 1615) by the Spanish writer, Miguel de Cervantes. It tells the story of a landowner (Quixote) who, attracted by tales of the knights of old, dresses up in armor and sets out to perform heroic deeds. The first part of the novel takes Quixote from his small village in La Mancha to the forests of the Sierra Morena, and then returns him to his village, where he recuperates from exhaustion and various injuries. The second part of the novel is more complex. Quixote is accompanied on his travels by his trusty servant, Sancho Panza. The purpose of this book is to teach how to read novels and how to discern the differences and similarities between the fiction and reality of experience itself.

WHO BECAME "THE MAGNIFICENT" OTTOMAN SULTAN?

In 1520, the greatest of the Ottoman rulers came to the throne. His name was Suleiman, and he was soon to become known as "The Magnificent" because of the splendor of his court and the might of his armies. His capital, Constantinople, renamed Istanbul, was the biggest city in the world. Suleiman set out to expand his empire even more. He captured cities as far apart as Belgrade, Baghdad, and Algiers, as well as Aden and the island of Rhodes. In 1526, he conqured the forces of the Hungarian king at the battle of Mohacz. Meanwhile, his navy, led by the pirate Barbarossa, ruled the Mediterranean.

Suleiman was not just a fine leader and warrior, he was also a poet and a scholar. Suleiman was known as *al-Qanuni*, "the law-giver." He had complete control over the daily lives of his subjects and chose slaves from his own bodyguard to govern provinces of the empire. He reformed the legal system so that land rents and taxes were collected properly. Even after his death in 1566, the Ottoman Empire continued to grow.

FACT FILE

The empire brought Suleiman great wealth, which he used to hire the best artists and architects. Among them was Mirman Sinan, who designed at least 165 mosques and palaces.

WHO FORMED THE "NEW MODEL ARMY"?

Oliver Cromwell (1599 to 1658), led the armed forces of Parliament to victory in the English Civil War against the royalists in the 1640s.

Cromwell was a military genius. In the winter of 1644 and 1645, when the war was at a stalemate, he got rid of the Parliamentarian high command of those who were not helping their cause. Cromwell's friends persuaded Parliament to establish a full-time professional force, called the New Model Army, under Sir Thomas Fairfax, with Cromwell as general. The New Model Army, or Roundheads, was a disciplined fighting force that never lost a major battle. On June 14, 1645, at the Battle of Naseby, in Northamptonshire, it destroyed the king's main field army. Cromwell deservedly earned the nickname "Ironsides."

FACT FILE

The term *Roundhead* originally referred to the parliamentary army, whose hair was cut short to fit their steel helmets, called *casques*. By the end of the English Civil War, the armies of Parliament were superior in cavalry and infantry.

WHO INTRODUCED PERESTROIKA AND GLASNOST?

What are *perestroika* and *glasnost*? They formed part of the policies of Mikhail Gorbachev, the last leader of the Soviet Union. After his appointment in 1985, Gorbachev proposed reforms of the Soviet political and economic system. Everything had been controlled from the center by the Communist Party. Gorbachev wanted to increase the power of elected bodies and modernize the economy. This program was called *perestroika*, or "restructuring." *Glasnost* means "openness," which he wanted the Soviet Union to have both internally and with other nations.

In 1990, Gorbachev received the Nobel Peace Prize for his reforms and arms limitations agreements with the United States. In 1991, the Soviet Union broke up.

FACT FILE

President Ronald Reagan was an avid supporter of Gorbachev's reform program in the USSR. In 1987, the two leaders signed an agreement to dismantle many kinds of nuclear weapons.

WHO WERE THE JAPANESE SHOGUNS?

The word *shogun* is Japanese for "great general." It was the title of the warrior rulers who led feudal Japan for nearly the whole period from 1192 to 1868.

In 1192, the emperor gave the title shogun to the military leader Yoritomo Minamoto, whose shogunate, or warrior government, was based in Kamakura. The Kamakura, or Minamoto, shogunate shared civil and military rule with the imperial court at Kyoto, although the emperors retained ceremonial and religious duties and rights. This shogunate collapsed in 1333. Five years later, a new shogunate was founded by the Ashikaga family in Kyoto. They were unable to maintain control, and the shogunate came to an end in 1568.

The following period saw battles for power among samurai. In 1603, Tokugawa Ieyasu became shogun of the whole country and took total control. Tokugawa policies were isolationist. Western trade and Christianity were banned, and Confucianism revived.

FACT FILE

Leyasu's shogunate was based in Edo, which is now Tokyo. His isolationist policies meant that very few westerners went to Japan for nearly 250 years.

WHO WAS NAPOLEON BONAPARTE?

FACT FILE

Napoleon's first wife was Josephine, the daughter of a planter from the French West Indies. She was intelligent and beautiful, but she and Napoleon had no children.

After years of political dispute and unrest, the French people welcomed Napoleon as their new leader in 1799. Not only was Napoleon a brilliant general, he also proved to be a skillful administrator. By 1812, he had created a French empire that covered almost all of Europe, but after being defeated in Russia in 1814, he was exiled to the island of Elba. He escaped in 1815, and the allies–Britain, Hanover, Belgium, and the Netherlands–responded to the threat.

The Battle of Waterloo, fought on June 18, 1815, near Brussels, Belgium, was Napoleon's final battle. Napoleon's army was routed, and he lost over 40,000 men. He was forced to abdicate, and the British sent him to the south Atlantic island of St. Helena, where he died in 1821.

WHO GAVE THE GETTYSBURG ADDRESS?

Abraham Lincoln (1809–1865) was the sixteenth president of the United States, and one of the greatest leaders in American history. A humane, far-sighted statesman in his lifetime, he became a legend and a folk hero after his death.

Lincoln delivered the short speech that has become known as the Gettysburg Address on November 19, 1863, at the site of the Civil War Battle of Gettysburg, in Pennsylvania. The occasion was a dedication ceremony for a cemetery for the Union soldiers who had died there in the three-day bloodbath four months earlier.

The purpose of the speech was to raise the spirits of the Union and to affirm the reasons why the Northern states were fighting the war against the Confederate states.

FACT FILE

Abraham Lincoln was against slavery. His election convinced the leaders of the Southern states that the only option to them was to leave the Union. South Carolina was the first state to leave in 1860, soon followed by Mississippi, Florida, Alabama, Georgia, and Louisiana.

WHO FOUNDED FASCISM?

Fascism was a political movement founded in Italy by Benito Mussolini (1883–1945) in 1919. His brand of revolutionary nationalism–nationalization and putting Italy's interests first–were popular with old soldiers. In 1921, he transformed the *Fasci di Combattimento* into the National Fascist Party. In 1922, his black-shirts marched on Rome and secured his appointment as prime minister. He imposed a one-party rule with himself as dictator.

He delayed involving Italy in World War II until 1940, when a German victory seemed probable. Five years later, after Italy's defeat, he was executed by Italian partisans.

FACT FILE

Sir Oswald Mosley formed the British Union of Fascists in 1932. His views were violently anti-Semitic, and his black-shirted followers rioted in areas with strong Jewish communities, such as London's East End. He was interned in World War II because of his support for Hitler.

WHO WAS REMBRANDT?

Rembrandt Harmenszoon van Rijn (1606–1669) was a Dutch baroque artist, who ranks as one of the greatest painters in the history of Western art. He is better known as Rembrandt. He had a deep understanding of human nature and a brilliant technique–not only in painting but in drawing and etching. His work made an enormous impact on his contemporaries and influenced the style of many later artists. Rembrandt was born in Leiden, the son of a miller. Despite coming from a family of modest means, his parents made sure he had a good education. Rembrandt began his studies at the Latin School, and at the age of 14, he was enrolled at the Leiden University.

FACT FILE

Leonardo da Vinci was one of the great Renaissance painters. His portrait of Mona Lisa is known throughout the world. Da Vinci was also a great inventor, recording ideas on subjects ranging from anatomy to geology. This is his painting called the Head of Leda.

WHO WAS ALEXANDER THE GREAT?

Alexander the Great (356–323 B.C.) was king of the Macedonians and was one of the greatest generals in history.
He came to the throne in 336 B.C., and after consolidating his power in Greece, began his conquest of the Persian Empire two years later. By 328 B.C., he had reached India, but a year later he had to turn back because his soldiers were threatening to mutiny after almost ten years away from home. Alexander's conquests furthered the exchange of Greek and Persian ideas and customs in western Asia and Egypt. His empire did not last beyond his death in Babylon in 323 B.C. It was split up into a number of smaller kingdoms, ruled by his friends and allies.

FACT FILE

Alexander was interested in promoting trade and commerce across his empire. This was made easier by imposing a single system of money throughout his lands.

WHO BUILT THE PARTHENON?

The ancient Greeks were pioneers in medicine, mathematics, and science. They looked at the world with logic and reason, and made some fundamental discoveries. In the year 432 B.C., a building called the Parthenon was completed. The Parthenon was built in Athens to honor the city's protector, the goddess Athene. Her statue, decorated in gold and ivory, was inside the great hall, enclosed by columns which supported the roof.

The Greeks built many beautiful temples to their gods. Stone columns, as used in the Parthenon, were a typical feature of many Greek buildings.

FACT FILE

Greek actors wore masks to show what kind of character (comic or tragic) they played. Audiences sat in the open air on a hillside to watch the plays.

WHO BUILT HADRIAN'S WALL?

Hadrian's Wall was built in 122 A.D. to defend the northern frontier of Roman Britain. It acted as a checkpoint between England and Scotland. The wall took eight years to build and stretches for 70 miles (118 km).

At this time, the Roman Empire was governed by the will of the emperor, but the emperor's power rested on his army. Weak or bad, emperors were sometimes overthrown by army generals. Some emperors ruled well. Hadrian, for example, traveled widely to inspect building projects. Others, such as Nero and Caligula, were cruel or mad. The Romans were such good organizers that the empire usually kept working even when the leadership was weak.

FACT FILE

Pictured is a Roman coin stamped with the head of the Emperor Hadrian. During his reign, he visited nearly every province in the Roman Empire.

WHO WERE THE SUFFRAGETTES?

During wartime, women were brought in to fill the jobs of those men who had gone to fight in the war. The poster shown here on the right emphasizes the important role women had to play. In 1893, New Zealand became the first country in the world to allow women to vote in national elections. Australia followed suit in 1903, Finland in 1906, and the United States in 1920. In other parts of the world, however, women were engaged in a bitter and often violent battle for the right to vote.

In Britain, Emmeline Pankhurst founded the Women's Social and Political Union in 1903. The WSPU believed in actions rather than words. Many of its members, known as *suffragettes*, were arrested and imprisoned. One suffragette, by the name of Emily Davison, was killed when she threw herself beneath the king's horse at a race.

FACT FILE

The women activists were frequently arrested for their actions, including Emmeline Pankhurst, shown here. The right to vote was extended to all women over the age of 21 in 1928. Emmeline Pankhurst died a month after British women gained equal voting rights.

WHO WAS GENGHIS KHAN?

Genghis Khan (1167–1227)

In 1167, a child named Temujin was born on the desolate plains of Mongolia. When the boy was nine, his father was murdered and his family was left poor and friendless. From this grim beginning, Temujin grew up to become one of the world's greatest conquerors. He was hailed by the Mongols as Genghis Khan, the "Universal Ruler."

In 1206, Genghis Khan became leader of all the Mongol people and began to build his astonishing empire. He was a ruthless warrior, destroying entire cities and their populations during his conquests. Yet he somehow succeeded in keeping the peace.

Although Genghis Khan died of a fever in 1227, the Mongols continued to build the empire he began.

FACT FILE

The Mongols lived on the flat, grassy, treeless areas of Asia, wandering with their herds of sheep, goats, and cattle. They carried their homes with them. The Mongols were tough and violent, and great horse riders.

Russian peasants working the land

WHO WAS THE MOST FAMOUS TSAR OF RUSSIA?

Peter the Great was a giant figure, well over 6-½ feet tall, and full of violent energy. When he became tsar of Russia in 1696, he was determined to use all his energy to make Russia a strong and modern state.

After many years of civil war, invasion, and bloodshed, Russia had just begun a slow progress out of its backward and primitive past. Under the new tsar, this progress became much quicker.

Peter himself spent years touring western Europe to find out how other countries were run. He was also a great builder. He built roads and canals, and introduced modern methods to mining and other industries.

FACT FILE

The beautiful city of St. Petersburg lies beside the River Neva. Its magnificent Winter Palace was the tsars' winter home. As a result of working in the difficult marshy conditions, thousands of peasants died while building Peter the Great's new city.

WHO DISCOVERED AUSTRALIA?

FACT FILE

In 1776, Cook set sail to find a sea passage from the Pacific around the north of America to the Atlantic. Ice blocked his way. He was the first European to reach Hawaii, where he was killed in 1779.

In 1768, the British government sent an expedition to find the mysterious southern continent. Its leader was James Cook, and his ship was a small but tough vessel, called Endeavor. After visiting the island of Tahiti, Cook sailed southwards and then west until he sighted an unknown land. It turned out to be what is now known as New Zealand. The Endeavor sailed on, searching for the east coast of Australia. By 1770, Cook reached the coast of Australia. He followed it northwards until he found a suitable place to land. He called this place Botany Bay. It is located on the southern border of what we know today as Sydney, Australia.

Cook's first meeting with the Maori people of New Zealand in 1769

WHO FIRST USED FURNITURE?

Although furniture must have existed earlier, the first real records of its use come from ancient Egypt. As we can tell from inscriptions and paintings in tombs, the wealthy Egyptians had beds, tables, chairs, stools, and chests by 2000 B.C. Similar furniture, dating from about 1350 B.C., was found in the tomb of the young eighteenth-dynasty pharaoh, Tutankhamun. It included storage chests, folding stools, beds, and an elaborate, richly decorated throne.

Elaborate furniture can also be seen in wall carvings depicting both Assyrian and Babylonian kings and queens. In these carvings they are shown reclining on high couches with footstools or sitting at high stands and tables to eat.

FACT FILE

Romans liked to fill their houses with furnishings, and the wealthy needed to store securely expensive items such as plates and clothing, as well as important documents. Sophisticated locks, for both storage chests and doors, date from the Roman period.

WHO INVENTED THE UMBRELLA?

No one is sure who first invented the umbrella, but in various forms it has been in use for more than 3,000 years. However, originally it was not used to keep the rain off but, rather, to protect the user from the heat of the sun. The first people to use sunshades were the Chinese, and these may have been made of lacquered paper. In time, using an umbrella became a status symbol, with only people in high office, especially royalty, being allowed to carry one. Some even had one carried over them.

Umbrellas were used as sunshades in ancient Egypt, Babylon, and Greece, while the Romans are thought to have been the first Europeans to use umbrellas to protect themselves against the rain.

The next records of umbrellas come from the late sixteenth century in southern Europe, again as a sunshade. During the next century, its use moved northwards.

The basic design of the umbrella has not changed much in 3,000 years, although such innovations as automatic- and compact-folding umbrellas have been made.

FACT FILE

Following the invention of plastic, other ways of protecting yourself from the rain are available; for example, this raincoat with a hood.

WHO BUILT THE TAJ MAHAL?

The Taj Mahal is a vast mausoleum near Agra, in India. It was built by the Mogul emperor Shah Jahan (1592–1666) in memory of his favorite wife, Mumtaz Mahal, who died in 1630. It took 20,000 skilled workers more than 20 years to complete its construction and decoration. The building is intended to represent the throne of God. It is the largest Islamic tomb ever built for a woman. The building stands on a marble platform 325 square feet and sits in a Persian water garden designed to represent paradise.

FACT FILE

Minarets, or towers, rise from each of the four corners of the Taj Mahal. The Taj itself soars another 200 feet into the air.

WHO FIRST USED STAMPS?

FACT FILE

Below is an example of a mailbox used in Great Britain. People mail their letters in this box, which will then be collected and sorted by the post office.

In the sixteenth century, governments began to have regular postal services. There were three reasons for doing this. One was to enable them to inspect suspicious correspondence, the second was to produce revenue, and the third was to provide a service for the public.

Henry VIII had a government postal service in England. In 1609, no one was allowed to carry letters except messengers authorized by the government. The whole system was finally changed in 1840.

Stamps were introduced and rates were made uniform for all distances within the country, varying only according to the weight of the piece of mail. All other countries modeled their postal systems on that of Great Britain.

WHO DREW THE FIRST CARTOON?

The word *cartoon* was originally used by painters and tapestry-makers during the Renaissance. However, this word referred to the final full-sized sketch of a large piece of work. Some of these "cartoons" still exist. The outlines of these designs are pricked with small holes. The cartoons were laid against the surface to be decorated, and charcoal powder was forced through these holes to transfer the design to it.

In the nineteenth century, newspapers and magazines started to use engraved drawings to make jokes and to illustrate news. These drawings also came to be called cartoons.

The first comic strips appeared in the early 1900s. Richard Outcault, the artist who created *Buster Brown*, published this comic strip in 1902. Ever since, newspapers have continued to run cartoon strips. Children's comic books also are popular.

FACT FILE

Before newspapers, famous caricaturists like Hogarth, Goya, Daumier, and Rowlandson made series of satirical engravings on themes of fashionable or political life, manners and morals. These engravings were widely circulated.

WHO MADE THE FIRST COMIC BOOK?

The *Yellow Kid*, created by Richard Felton Outcault in 1895, is recognized as the first comic book.

Early forms of this sequential art can be seen in Paleolithic cave drawings, made by prehistoric man almost 20,000 years ago.

The terms *comics* and *comic strips* became established around 1900 in the United States when all strips were indeed comic. Comic strips created from wood blocks date back to 1550.

A comic book is a bound collection of strips, typically telling a single story or a series of different stories. Most of the better newspaper strips eventually appear in book form as well.

FACT FILE

Richard Felton Outcault was the first person to use the caption bubble, or balloon, the space where what the characters say is written.

Before the advent of Superhero comic books were Funny Books. People called them "funny" books because inside were reprints of comic strips from newspapers, such as the *Peanuts* cartoon today.

WHO WERE THE SUMERIANS?

About 7,000 years ago, farmers began to move into an area of land between the Tigris and the Euphrates Rivers. This fertile land was called Mesopotamia, in what is now called Iraq. In the south of Mesopotamia was the land known as Sumer. The Sumerians, as they became known, were a very inventive race. They developed the first form of writing and recording numbers.

The Sumerians drew pictures on soft clay with a pointed reed. The pictures were drawn downwards in lines, beginning with the right-hand side. Later, they started to write across the tablet from left to right. The reed tip became wedge-shaped, as did the marks it made.

FACT FILE

Reed houses were built using reeds cut down from the marshes around the Tigris and Euphrates Rivers. The Sumerians also made canoes from these reeds.

WHO INVENTED THE WHEEL?

FACT FILE

The wheel was first used by the Sumerians to make pottery about 3500 B.C. Around 300 years later, this invention was adapted for a startling new use–that of transportation.

The Sumerians were also credited for the revolutionary invention of the wheel and the plough. They grew bumper crops of cereals, which they traded for items they needed: wood, building stone, or metals. Wheeled carts and their writing skills helped them to develop long-distance trade.

The first wheels were made of planks of solid wood held together with crosspieces. They were clumsy and heavy at the beginning. In time, lighter wheels were made, which had many spokes. The first ploughs were also made of wood with the blade made from bronze.

WHO WAS BOUDICCA?

Boudicca, also known as Boadicea, was the queen of the Iceni, a tribe of Celts living in eastern England. Her husband was a governor, who worked with the Romans. After his death, the Romans tried to take control. Boudicca led a rebellion, which raided the towns of Colchester and London, until the Roman armies marched against her. The Romans defeated the Iceni and their Celtic allies. She is renowned for fighting from a chariot. The Romans had to develop special tactics to combat these fast-moving warriors. Boudicca ended her life by taking poison to avoid being captured.

FACT FILE

Here is an example of Celtic poetry:

Storm at Sea
Tempest on the plain of Lir
Bursts its barriers far and near
And upon the rising tide
Wind and noisy winter ride
Winter throws a shining spear.

Queen Boudicca on her chariot

WHO WERE THE CELTS?

The Celts came from central Europe, although their previous origins are unclear. Around 500 B.C., perhaps to escape wars with their Germanic neighbors, they began to move westward. Groups of people settled in what are now Spain, France, Britain, and Ireland. Celts were war-like and their arrival usually led to fighting.

The Celts were artistic people. They loved stories and music. They made beautiful jewelery and metalwork, decorated with abstract designs and animal shapes.

They had no written language. They passed on their legends of gods and heroes in stories around the fire. Most of what we know of the Celts today comes from the writings of their enemies, such as the Romans. The Celts themselves left a legacy of art, legend, and language. Welsh, Breton, Cornish, Irish, and Scottish Gaelic are all Celtic languages.

FACT FILE

The Celts often constructed their settlements on hilltops, which could be easily defended. These settlements are identified by circular defensive ditches that still survive in former Celtic areas.

An example of Celtic art

How?

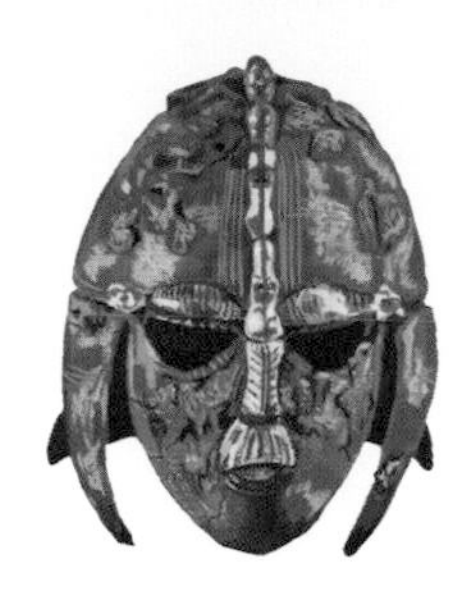

CONTENTS

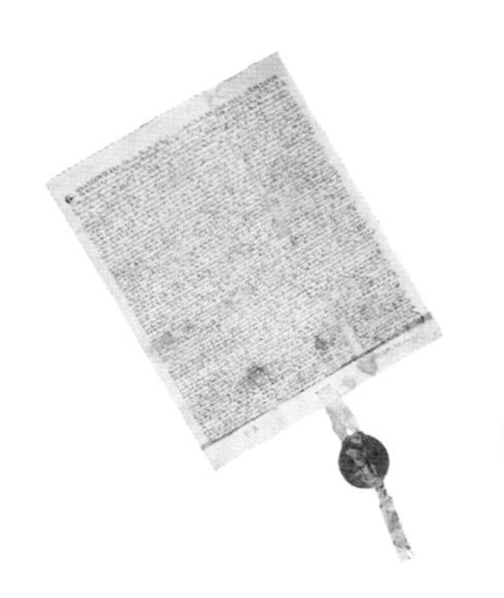

How do archaeologists reconstruct the past?

An archaeologist reconstructs the past by studying buildings and objects that have survived. Sometimes historical remains are astonishingly well preserved. For example, the Roman cities of Pompeii and Herculaneum were caught off guard by the eruption of Mount Vesuvius. Many tiny aspects of Roman life were preserved, including graffiti on the walls. Such perfect preservation is very rare.

Archaeologists usually need to make a painstaking reconstruction, carefully excavating the remains of ruined buildings. Sometimes, only the post-holes of a wooden building are left, but even they can provide useful clues about the type of building. The oldest archaeological remains come from the Stone Age. The remains of flint tools and weapons have survived, together with bones that show which animals were hunted and eaten.

FACT FILE

This is Trajan's column, part of a giant monument that the Roman emperor Trajan built to record his deeds. It shows the day-to-day tasks of the Roman army.

Newly cut wood begins to lose its radiocarbon.

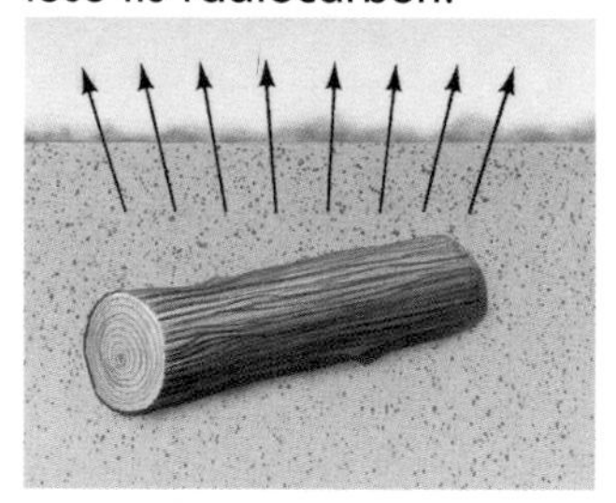

After 5,700 years, it has lost half its radiocarbon.

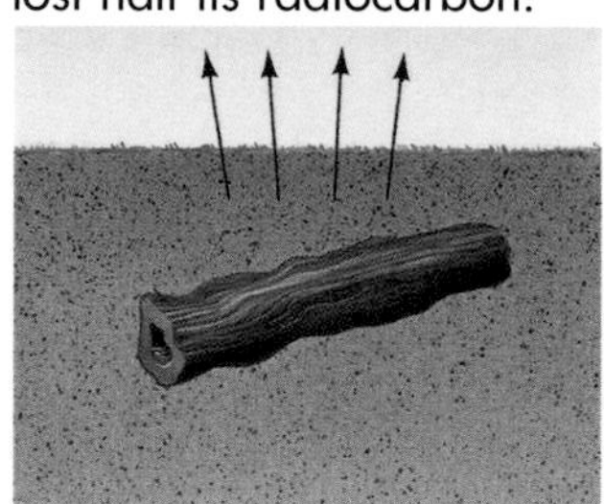

After 5,700 more years, it has lost half as much again.

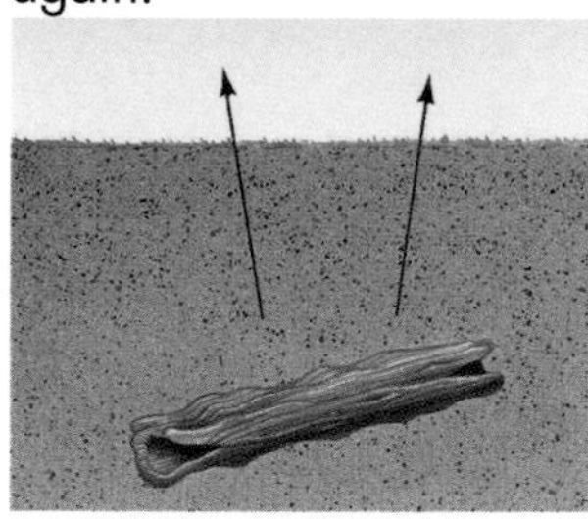

Carbon, which forms a part of living things, loses its radioactivity at a steady and predictable rate. Archaelogists use this information to determine the age of organic remains. After about 70,000 years, organic material has lost all of its radiocarbon. Carbon dating is used by archaeologists to help determine the age of artifacts.

HOW DO ARCHAEOLOGISTS KNOW WHAT THEY FIND?

An archaeologist does not always find the things he or she needs to build a complete picture of a people or a way of life. After all, what the archaeologist finds is only what people left behind, usually everyday objects. These might be remains of houses, tools, jewelery, dishes, toys, and bones of animals used for food. Objects made of leather, wood, cloth, wool, or straw usually decay and leave no trace. But despite this, the archaeologist can still tell us a great deal. He or she first finds out the order in which early towns were built, one upon the ruins of another. Then the archaeologist must know the town in which each object was found. Each object is labeled, photographed, and measured. If the site belonged to historic times, the archaeologist must know the ancient writing used in that place. There are many experts who help archaeologists, such as geologists, botanists, and zoologists, all of whom help identify and analyze what they have found. Sometimes, it takes years of work and study before the archaeologists are ready to publish what they have found.

FACT FILE

This iron helmet was part of a series of treasures and artifacts unearthed at a burial site called Sutton Hoo, in Suffolk, England.

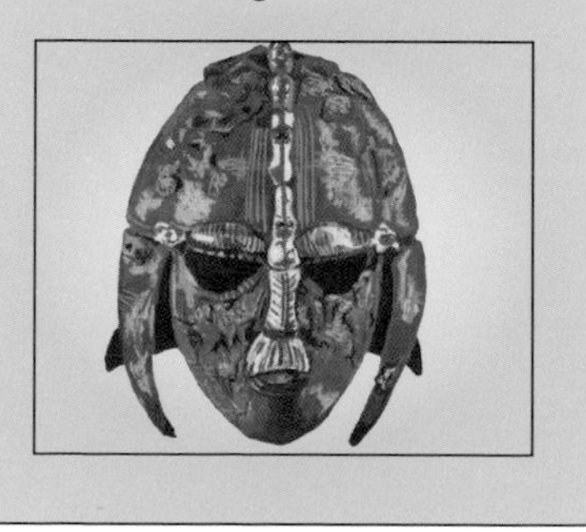

HOW WERE THE EGYPTIAN PYRAMIDS BUILT?

Pyramid-building developed slowly in ancient Egypt. The first pyramids were simple structures called *mastabas*, which were platforms built over the tombs of important people. Over the years, further levels were added, until a structure called a *step pyramid* was produced.

In later pyramids, the steps were filled in to produce the smooth conical shape of the famous Pyramids at Giza, which we can see today. Pyramid-building became an important part of the Egyptian civilization. Egyptians believed that the pyramids offered a pathway to heaven for their rulers, the pharaohs, who were buried with items that they might need for the afterlife.

FACT FILE

Civilizations sprang up at similar times in different parts of the world. One very advanced civilization was in the Indus Valley, in modern Pakistan and India.

HOW WERE HIEROGLYPHICS UNDERSTOOD?

No one really knows how the first writing system developed because no records remain. The earliest known writing was recorded in the form of picture symbols on clay tablets by the ancient Sumerians around 3500 B.C.

Hieroglyphics was a system of writing used by the ancient Egyptians around 3000 B.C., using drawings rather than the shapes we use in modern writing. They gradually became more stylized to resemble modern forms of writing.

The discovery of the Rosetta Stone, which contained the same inscription in hieroglyphics, demotic script, and Greek, allowed the meaning of the complicated pictures to be understood.

It is likely that all writing started this way, before shapes and letters were used to indicate sounds.

FACT FILE

Ancient Egyptian hieroglyphic writing had long been indecipherable. The discovery of the Rosetta stone provided the key to understanding this ancient script.

How was Rome founded?

According to legend, Rome was founded in 753 B.C. by twin brothers Romulus and Remus. The babies were raised by a she-wolf, having been abandoned by their uncle on the banks of the Tiber River. They were eventually rescued by a shepherd.

By 509 B.C., the original Etruscan inhabitants of Rome had been driven out, and by 275 B.C., Rome controlled most of Italy. The Phoenicians were great rivals of Rome. They were finally defeated by the Romans in the Punic Wars (261–146 B.C.). After this, the Romans were able to extend their empire with little organized resistance. The Celts, the Seleucid kings, the Greeks, and the Egyptians all fell before Roman power. Only the Parthians in the East and the Germanic tribes in Northwest Europe defied the mighty Roman army.

FACT FILE

This photo shows part of the complex of Roman baths in the city of Bath, in England. Romans visited the public baths to bathe in hot and cold pools, and to relax and talk with their friends.

HOW VAST WAS THE ROMAN EMPIRE?

FACT FILE

The disciplined Roman armies developed special weapons and techniques to overcome the tribes they encountered as the empire expanded. This "tortoise" formation proved unconquerable against their Celtic foes.

At its peak, the Roman army extended all around the Mediterranean Sea, as well as most of the rest of Europe. Much of what is now England, France, Belgium, the Netherlands, Spain, Portugal, Switzerland, Austria, Hungary, part of Germany, Romania, Bulgaria, Greece, Turkey, Israel, Syria, Arabia, Tunisia, Algeria, and Morocco was ruled by the Romans from their base in Italy.

A huge army was needed to maintain control over these regions, and the costs were tremendous. There were continual minor wars and skirmishes along the edges of the Empire, which meant that large garrisons of soldiers had to be quartered there.

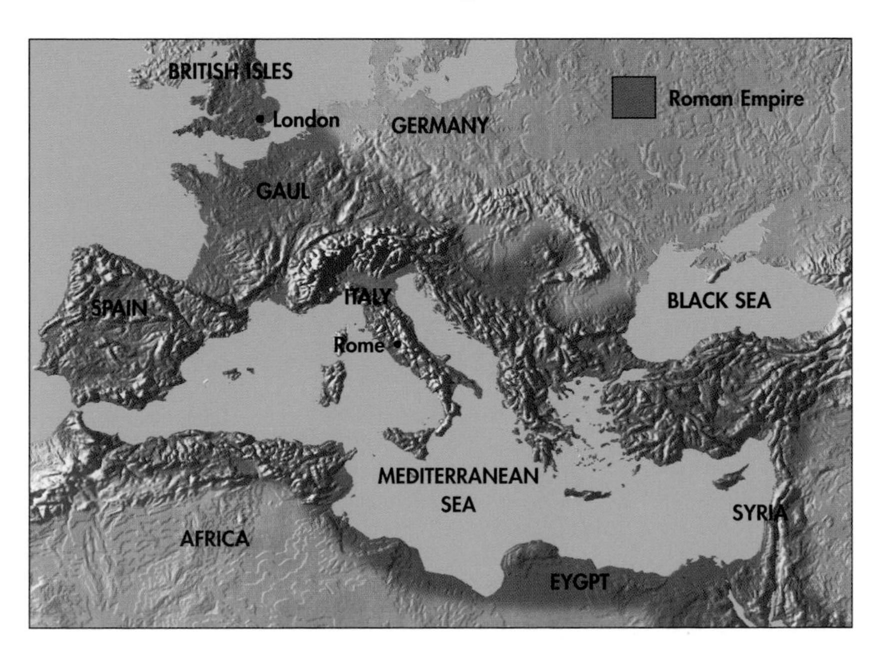

HOW SUCCESSFUL WERE VIKING ATTACKS?

The Vikings came from Scandinavia, which includes the countries we know today as Norway, Denmark, and Sweden. Their homeland of mountains, fjords, and forests offered little spare farmland for a growing population, so many Vikings went abroad in search of new lands to settle.

They were fierce warriors, and their first impact on western Europe was a violent one. Norwegians and Danes began to sail across the North Sea in the late 700s A.D., raiding the coasts of Britain and mainland Europe. They attacked churches and towns, carrying off loot and slaves. Their raids caused panic, and the rulers tried to buy off these invaders with gold, known as *Danegeld*. This only encouraged the Vikings to come back for more.

In Britain, the Vikings were finally defeated by Alfred, the king of Wessex.

FACT FILE

Religion was important to the Vikings. Their most important gods were Odin, Thor, and Gray. Odin, the god of battle, was the leader of the Norse gods. He lived in a place called Valhalla.

HOW FAR DID THE VIKINGS TRAVEL?

FACT FILE

The Viking longships were fast and strong enough to cross oceans. They had a long, slender hull with a single mast and sail.

At a time when sailors dared not venture far from the coasts, the Vikings boldly sailed across the Atlantic in their small, open longships. Viking trade routes took them throughout Europe and beyond. The Vikings traveled as far east as Baghdad and Istanbul, and as far west as Greenland and Canada. Wherever Vikings landed, they mingled with local people and began to set up colonies in Iceland and Greenland, and later in North America. Traces of Viking settlements have been found in Maine and in Newfoundland. However, these colonies soon vanished, together with the colony in Greenland. Other Vikings sailed around the Mediterranean, trading for goods from places as far away as China.

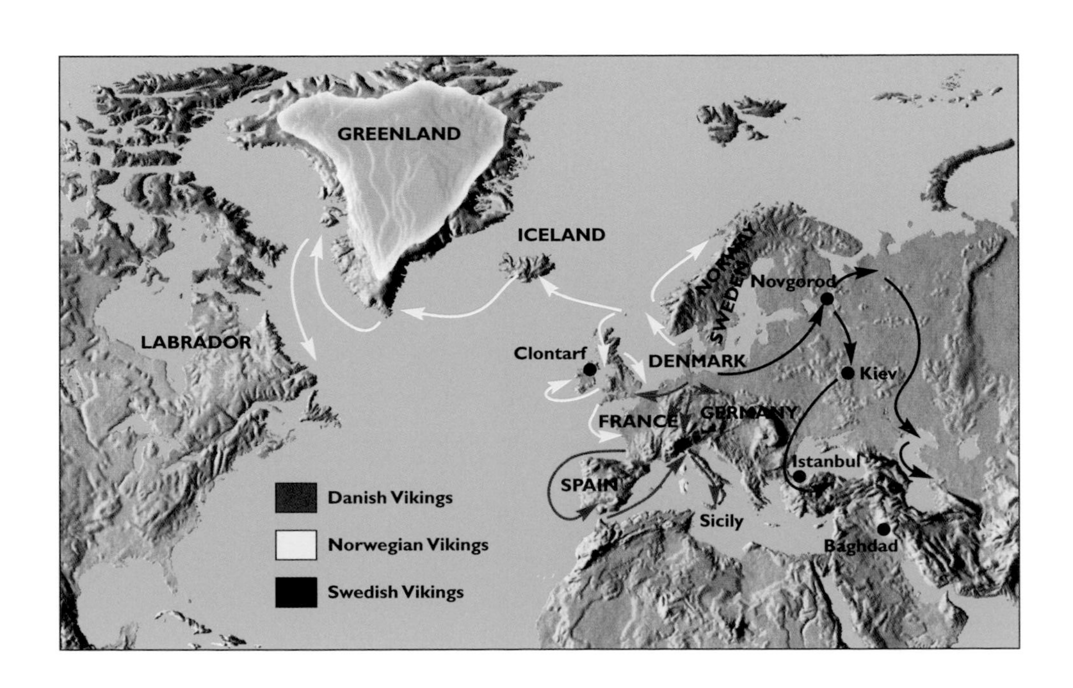

HOW IS CONFUCIUS REMEMBERED?

Confucius

Confucius was an ancient Chinese philosopher who taught the need for moral responsibility and virtue. His teachings did not make much impact during his lifetime, but they later became the central part of Chinese moral and religious thinking.

Confucius lived around 551 to 479 B.C, in the time of the Zhou dynasty. The Zhou was the longest-lasting group of Chinese rulers, who governed the country from 1122 to 256 B.C.

Confucianism was probably the most important feature in Chinese life until the appearance of Communism in the twentieth century. Confucianism resembles a religion, but instead of worshiping gods it is a guide to morality and good government.

Although Confucius lived thousands of years ago, his influence in everyday life is still strong in China today.

FACT FILE

The oldest printed book known is the *Diamond Sutta*, a Buddhist scroll made from sheets of paper printed with woodblocks. It was made in China in 868 A.D.

HOW WERE THE TERRACOTTA WARRIORS MADE?

FACT FILE

The Chinese admired the swift horses of the central Asian grassy plain so much that they made bronze statuettes of "flying horses."

In China, the powerful Qin dynasty came to power in the third century B.C. They quickly conquered their neighbors to form a large empire covering most of modern China. The Qin emperor Shi Huangdi standardized weights and measures, and introduced a single form of currency. He is best remembered for his construction of the Great Wall of China, which stretches for 1,400 miles across northern China.

When the emperor died, a huge tomb was built to hold his body. It was filled with a guardian army of thousands of life-sized terracotta, or pottery, warriors. Each figure was individually molded. The figures were placed in three pits inside the large complex surrounding the emperor's tomb.

HOW DID THE NORMANS CHANGE BRITAIN?

The Bayeux tapestry records the Norman victory over the Saxon King Harold, who is shown here receiving a fatal arrow in his eye.

FACT FILE

Knights were soldiers in the service of a Norman lord. They owed their loyalty to their lord and had to fight for him whenever asked. This meant that the knights were called upon in times of unrest.

The Normans introduced the feudal system to England. According to this system, the king owned all the land. Others could hold land in exchange for providing services to the king. William the Conqueror appointed barons, who were provided with estates taken from the original English earls. In return, the barons paid him taxes and supplied soldiers for his armies.

The barons, in turn, let their knights hold smaller sections of land, while the knights rented part of this land to people called *villeins*. These were farmers who had to provide some of their produce to the local lord of the manor. In this way, the land and all of English society was broken down into small, easily controlled units.

HOW DOES THE DOMESDAY BOOK HELP HISTORIANS?

The Domesday Book

Once the Normans had secured their hold over their new territory, they wanted to know exactly what it was worth. In 1085 A.D., William I ordered a survey of land in England. These findings were reported in the *Domesday Book*, which means "Day of Judgment." It is the best record we have of life in England between 1066 and 1088 A.D. It names about 13,000 towns and villages.

This book listed every town, village, and farm, who owned what and how much each hold was worth, so that taxes could be applied. This book is still in existence today.

FACT FILE

Conwy castle, in north Wales, is typical of the castles built by the Normans. It was built to give defending archers a clear field of fire against any attackers, and it could withstand a long siege.

How did the Mongols live?

The Mongols never settled permanently but lived in large, circular tent-like prefabricated homes called *yurts*.

These homes were carried with them during their migrations and invasions, and they are still used today. They are made of felt, which is fastened over a light, wooden frame. The whole structure can be dismantled quickly and carried by horses as the Mongol tribes would migrate across the steppes, or grassy plains, following their grazing flocks.

The Mongols were feared for their unpredictable attacks on cities throughout Asia and the Middle East. Genghis Khan was a famous Mongol who unified the scattered tribes, and began the conquest that resulted in the Mongols controlling nearly all of Asia and threatening to destroy Europe. After the death of Genghis' grandson, Kublai, the Empire proved too large to govern and began to break up.

This is an example of a Mongol home, called a *yurt*, which they carried with them during their migrations and invasions.

HOW EXTENSIVE WAS THE MONGOL EMPIRE?

The vast Mongol empire stretched across central Asia from the Sea of Japan to the Caspian Sea and occupied most of modern Russia. The Mongols succeeded against established armies because they were unpredictable. They charged into battle on horseback, relying entirely on speed and surprise, and took no prisoners. The Mongols were remorseless fighters, developing fighting machines that enabled them to break into the cities they raided. They were merciless towards those who resisted them, and sometimes slaughtered entire populations. Most cities surrendered immediately, rather than risk being massacred.

FACT FILE

Marco Polo was one of the first Europeans to travel through Mongol territory. His reports helped to establish trade routes there.

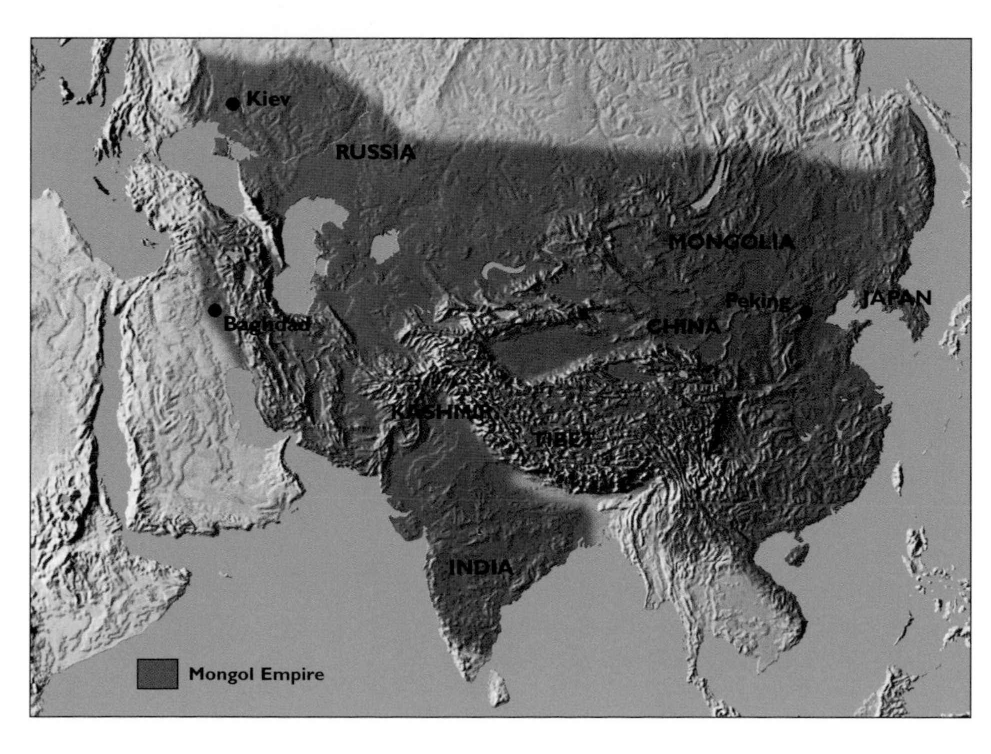

HOW LONG WAS THE HUNDRED YEARS WAR?

The Hundred Years War began in 1337 and continued for more than a century. It was not a single war but a series of skirmishes between England and France. It began when the English tried to dominate France. The French, in turn, tried to confiscate lands occupied by the English.

The English invaded France and won a great battle at Crécy. The British archers with their longbows defeated a much larger army of knights, marking the beginning of the end for mounted knights. Further battles followed. But in 1396, Richard II of England married the daughter of Charles VI of France, establishing a 20-year truce that finally ended the fighting.

FACT FILE

The two branches of the Plantagenet family battled for the throne in the Wars of the Roses from 1455–1485. The name comes from the red rose of Lancaster and the white Rose of York.

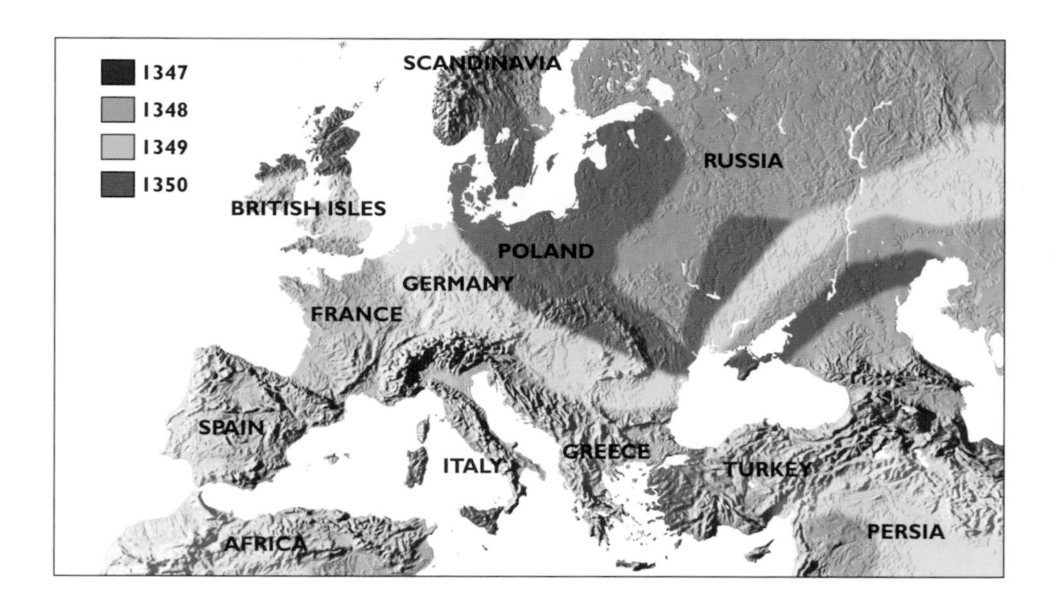

HOW WIDESPREAD WAS THE BLACK DEATH?

The Black Death was an epidemic that permanently changed the face of medieval Europe. It killed more than one-quarter of the population, causing thousands of villages to be abandoned and then disappear.

The Black Death probably came to Europe from Central Asia by way of Mongol raiders. The first epidemics began in Italy, in 1347, and spread rapidly through the rest of Europe.

The disease was spread by flea bites from infected rats, but because its cause was not known, the infection raged unchecked. The shortage of manual workers that resulted led to the collapse of the long-established feudal system.

FACT FILE

To try and ward off The Black Death, people burned incense, believing that the disease was transmitted in the air. Towns also rang their church bells or fired cannons, in a futile attempt to drive the plague away with sound.

How did the Spanish Empire develop?

After the Americas were discovered, Spanish adventurers set out to seek their fortunes. They sent expeditions to South and Central America and to Mexico in search of gold and treasure. In Mexico, a group of Spanish soldiers attacked the capital of the Aztec Empire. The Aztecs had been expecting the god Quetzalcoatl to return to earth and believed that the leader of the raiders, Cortés, was this god. The Aztecs offered little resistance, so Cortés captured Montezuma, the Aztec emperor, and ruled in his place. In Peru, the adventurer Pizarro took advantage of a civil war to conquer the Incas, murdering their rulers.

Several factors made it easy for a small group of Spaniards to conquer these great civilizations. Though vastly outnumbered, the Spanish had horses, armor, and guns, which gave them a huge advantage over the native warriors.

FACT FILE

Other nations expanded their empires in the same way as the Spanish. Many British people, known as *pilgrims*, sailed to America to establish themselves and settle on this newly discovered land.

HOW WAS THE SPANISH *ARMADA* DEFEATED?

The English were envious of Spain's rich colonies in South and Central America. During the reign of Elizabeth I, the English raided Spanish ships carrying gold and silver to Spain. The Spanish suspected that English royalty supported these privateers, which angered them. To make matters worse, an English army helped the Dutch, who were fighting against Spanish rule. In 1588, Philip II of Spain sent the Spanish *Armada* to invade England. The Spanish came close to conquering England at this time. Their ship, however, was scattered by storms, then raided and destroyed by English ships.

FACT FILE

Ships such as these were used for the voyages pilgrims made in search of a new life, as they headed from England to America.

HOW DID A SPIDER HELP ROBERT THE BRUCE?

Robert the Bruce (1274–1329) was a gallant Scottish king. After claiming the throne in 1306, he spent most of his reign trying to free his country from English rule. A legend is told about Bruce hiding from his enemies. He was lying on a bed in a hut when he saw a spider trying to swing itself from one beam to another by one of its threads. It tried six times and failed. Bruce realized that he had fought the same number of battles in vain against the English. He decided that if the spider tried a seventh time and succeeded, he would also try again. The spider's seventh attempt was successful, so Bruce took heart and went forth to victory.

Within two years, he had gained control of nearly all of Scotland. Then he advanced into England, destroying everything in his path. In 1314, the English invaded Scotland, but Bruce's forces defeated them in the Battle of Bannockburn. Edward III finally recognized Scotland's independence and the right of Bruce to the throne as King Robert I, in 1328.

FACT FILE

Over 10,000 English soldiers were killed at the Battle of Bannockburn. After this victory, Bruce had driven the English out of Scotland.

HOW IS FRANCISCO PIZARRO REMEMBERED?

In the mid-1520s, a Spanish adventurer by the name of Francisco Pizarro began to explore the west coast of South America. He had heard tales of the Inca empire and its treasures of silver and gold. About 1527, Pizarro and a few of his followers landed near the Inca city of Tumbes, on Peru's north coast. They became the first white men to set foot in Peru. Pizarro saw enough riches at Tumbes to convince him that the legends about the Inca were true. He returned in 1532 with about 180 men, who were later joined by other Spanish troops. By the end of 1533, the Spanish had easily conquered most of Peru, including the fabulous city of Cusco, the Inca capital. In 1535, Pizarro founded Lima, which became the core of the Spanish government in South America.

FACT FILE

By 1550, Spain ruled most of Central and South America and the West Indies. Fleets of Spanish galleons carried gold and silver, and plundered treasures across the Atlantic to Europe.

How did the United States become independent?

Resentment against taxes imposed on the American colonies by Britain led to the Declaration of Independence in 1776. In the following war, called the Revolutionary War, the Americans finally gained full independence of British rule.

The new American nation that resulted consisted of 13 states, which has now grown to 50. It had a president, who would be elected every four years, and was run by a Congress. This same structure exists today.

FACT FILE

Eleven Confederate states (orange) broke away from the Union (green), fearing that slavery would be abolished. Five slave states (red) stayed in the Union, although some of their inhabitants supported the Confederacy.

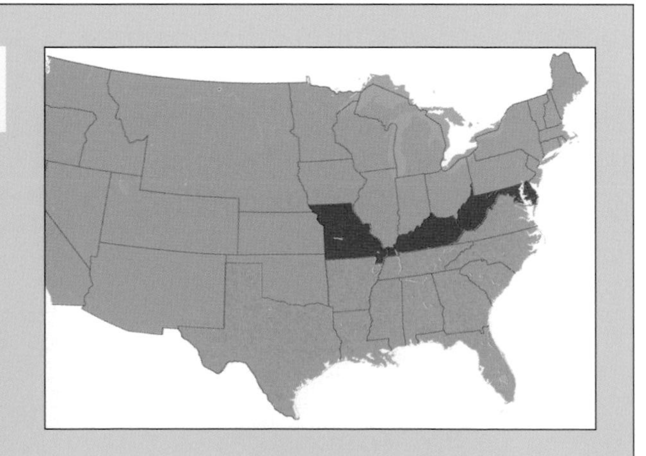

HOW DID THE AMERICAN INDIANS LOSE THEIR LAND?

FACT FILE

The American flag was originally designed with 13 stars and 13 stripes to represent the the original 13 colonies that signed the Declaration of Independence. With each new state, another star has been added to the flag.

The Native American Indians understandably resented the numbers of settlers who invaded their traditional hunting and grazing lands. As the population of the United States grew, the Indians were forced to migrate to the south and west. Soon they had nowhere left to go and began to fight back.

The United States government reacted by forcing the American Indians into reservations on land that the settlers did not want. Many Indians died fighting to save their land or from starvation and disease.

The huge herds of buffalo on which many Indians depended were hunted by the settlers, depriving the Indians of their main source of food, clothing, and shelter. Today, many Indian tribes continue to live on reservations in Arizona and New Mexico.

HOW DID AFRICA BECOME COLONIZED?

FACT FILE

Powerful tribes, such as the Zulus, mounted strong resistance to the invading colonial armies.

The central regions of Africa were not well explored until the middle of the 1800s. As the continent was explored, it was colonized by European countries seeking territories to exploit and bring them riches.

The British, Dutch, French, and Portuguese all established colonies near the coast and later inland. The slave trade had destroyed the structure of many once-powerful African nations, and they were unable to resist the Europeans with their modern weapons. Germany, Belgium, and Italy all joined in the scramble to capture new lands in Africa.

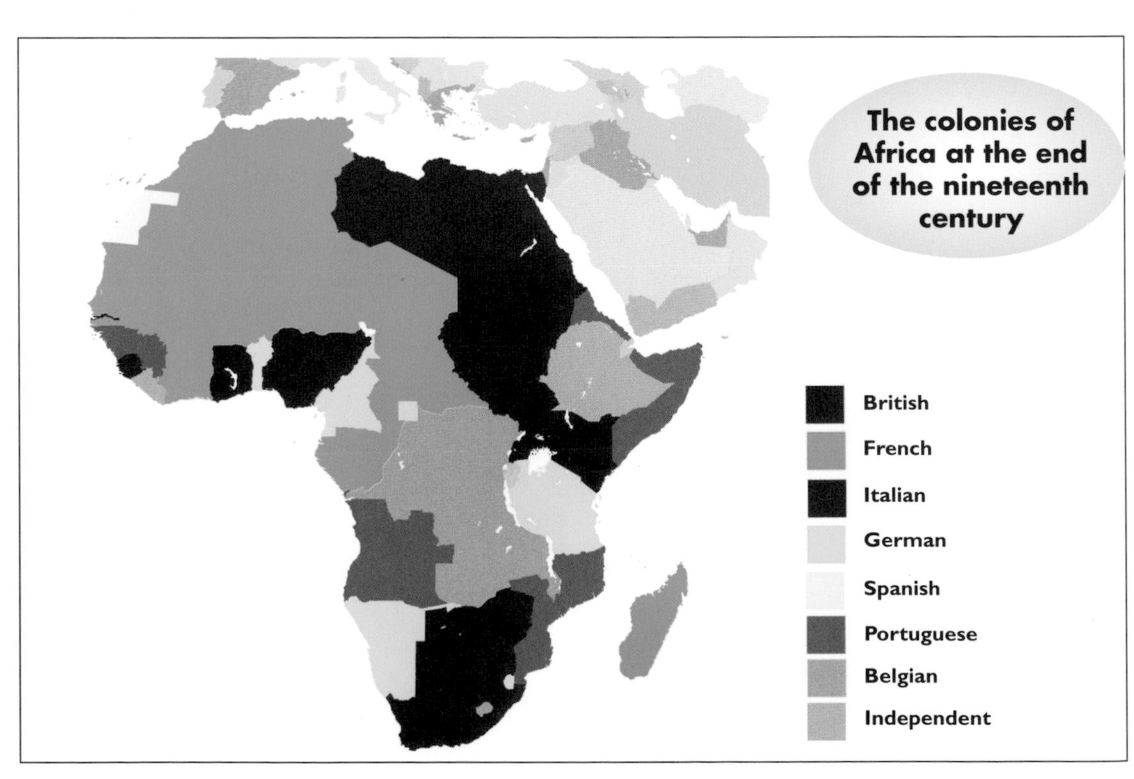

The colonies of Africa at the end of the nineteenth century

How did Britain gain Hong Kong?

For centuries, China was a closed country and foreigners were not encouraged to explore it. European traders smuggled large amounts of opium into China so that people became addicted and would pay for the opium with silver. The Chinese government tried to stop this opium trade, but the British sent their navy to threaten them. From 1839 to 1842, the British and Chinese fought over access to the Chinese ports. The Chinese were defeated, and the British forced them to grant trading rights. Five ports were opened, and Hong Kong Island became a British colony. In 1898, Britain was given Hong Kong on a 99-year lease, during which time it became a hugely successful center of finance and trade.

FACT FILE

Hong Kong was not Britain's only colony. By the middle of the eighteenth century, the British empire had reached every corner of the globe, as this map shows.

HOW DID THE FRENCH REVOLUTION BEGIN?

On July 14, 1789, a mob attacked the royal prison in Paris, the Bastille. Although only a few prisoners were released, this event marked the end of royal power in France and began the Revolution.

FACT FILE

Napoleon was a very effective military leader and politician. He ruled France for 15 years, expanding their empire abroad.

During the eighteenth century, France was not prosperous. The government was short of money and needed to raise its taxes. Louis XVI could do this only by recalling a traditional assembly, which promptly demanded political reforms. He responded by trying to dismiss the assembly, but the citizens of Paris revolted in support of the assembly.

The new National Assembly showed its strength by introducing new laws in 1791, insisting on freedom and equality. The royal family was imprisoned at first, then tried and executed.

How did the guillotine become feared?

The French Revolution was opposed by neighboring countries in the fear that the unrest would spread across Europe. A Committee of Public Safety was set up in France to defend the revolution. They executed any person who might oppose this Committee. In fact, thousands of people who were thought to threaten this new regime were put to death by the recently invented guillotine.

This period became known as the Reign of Terror. It lasted for about a year. During this time, around 18,000 people were put to death. The French aristocracy was almost entirely wiped out, along with any political opponents of the regime. The Reign of Terror finally came to an end when the head of the Committee of Public Safety, Robespierre, was accused of treason.

FACT FILE

Marie Antoinette, wife of Louis XVI, was an influential woman in the court. She met a gruesome death, beheaded on the guillotine.

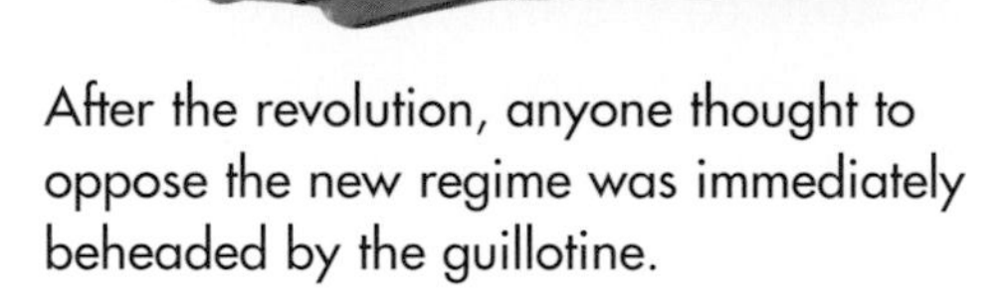

After the revolution, anyone thought to oppose the new regime was immediately beheaded by the guillotine.

How did the Industrial Revolution change Britain?

In the early eighteenth century, Britain was still a large agricultural nation. The few manufactured goods were made in small workshops or at home. As a result of Britain's world trading, the cotton industry developed and everything changed. At first, water power was used to drive spinning and weaving machines, and factories and mills were set up. New towns were built to provide homes for the workers. Steam engines were adapted to provide power to factories. The railway and canal system were developed. The other key development was the smelting of iron using coke, rather than wood. Britain was able to exploit the raw materials from her overseas empire to become one the world's most prosperous industrial nations.

FACT FILE

Trade with the Far East involved a long voyage around the tip of Africa. The Suez Canal provided a quick route from the Mediterranean to the Red Sea.

HOW SIGNIFICANT WAS THE INVENTION OF THE STEAM ENGINE?

The invention of the steam engine was a significant advancement in the eighteenth century, providing power for the Industrial Revolution. The first steam engines were massive stationary devices that pumped water from flooded mines, but they were soon adapted to power vessels.

The first steam locomotives appeared in the early nineteenth century. They carried goods and allowed people to travel to factories where they worked. Trains were an important means of social change because, for the first time, people could travel quickly and visit places that were previously too far away.

FACT FILE

Steam locomotion also made overseas trading possible. One of the most important exports was tea, which was in great demand in Europe.

How did World War I begin?

Continual trouble in the Balkans led to the formation of several complicated military alliances throughout Europe. The continent was eventually split into two groups. Britain, France, and later Russia joined to form the *Entente Cordiale*; while Germany, Austria-Hungary, and Italy formed the *Triple Alliance*. In 1914, Archduke Franz Ferdinand of Austria-Hungary was assassinated in Serbia, activating the alliance agreements. First, Austria declared war on Serbia, Russia sided with Serbia, and then Germany declared war on Russia. Germany invaded Belgium, drawing the British and French into the conflict.

FACT FILE

The Versailles Treaty ended World War I, but its terms were so severe that Germany suffered economic collapse. This caused resentment that built up and eventually contributed to the causes of World War II.

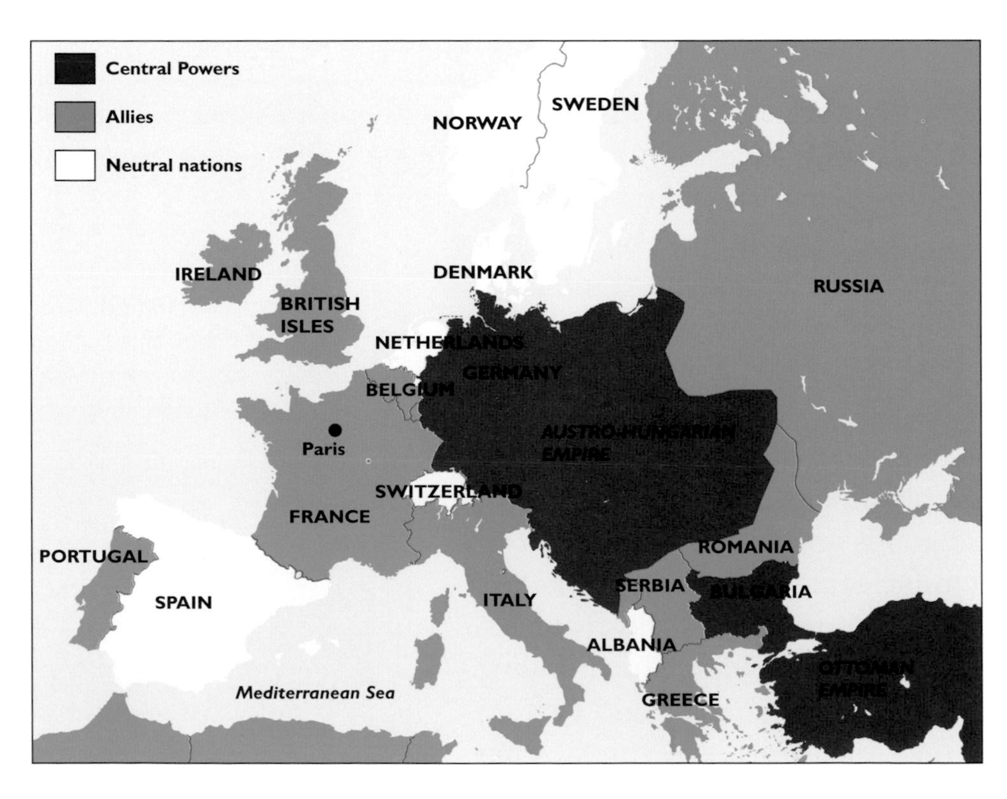

How did new technology influence World War I?

World War I was the first mechanized war in history. In the beginning, fighting was similar to wars fought in the previous century. But new and terrifying weapons were introduced, which completely changed the whole style of warfare.

Aircraft were used for the first time to observe the enemy and to locate suitable targets for the long-range artillery. Later on, fighter planes began to shoot down the spotters, introducing aerial warfare. Aircraft and Zeppelin airships were used as bombers.

The most terrifying new weapon was poison gas, used by both sides. It caused millions of deaths and terrible suffering. Tanks also made their first appearance.

FACT FILE

The war brought the first armored tanks into battle. They could break through enemy lines and create openings for troops. Earlier use of tanks could have saved lives and helped shorten the war.

HOW DID WORLD WAR II BEGIN?

FACT FILE

Britain was led through World War II by Winston Churchill. He is remembered for his great wartime leadership qualities. He is also remembered for his famous "V for victory" sign.

As in World War I, some international alliances were activated following the German invasion of Poland. As a result of this, Britain and France declared war on Germany.

When the Germans attacked Poland, the Russians also attacked the country, and it was divided.

The Germans went on to invade Denmark, Norway, Belgium, The Netherlands, and France in quick succession. They crushed any resistance with overwhelming armored forces.

World War II killed more people than any other war in history. The fighting spread to nearly every part of the world and included nearly 60 nations.

The United States entered the war in 1941 after being attacked by Germany's ally, Japan. The United States was led through World War II by its President, Franklin Roosevelt.

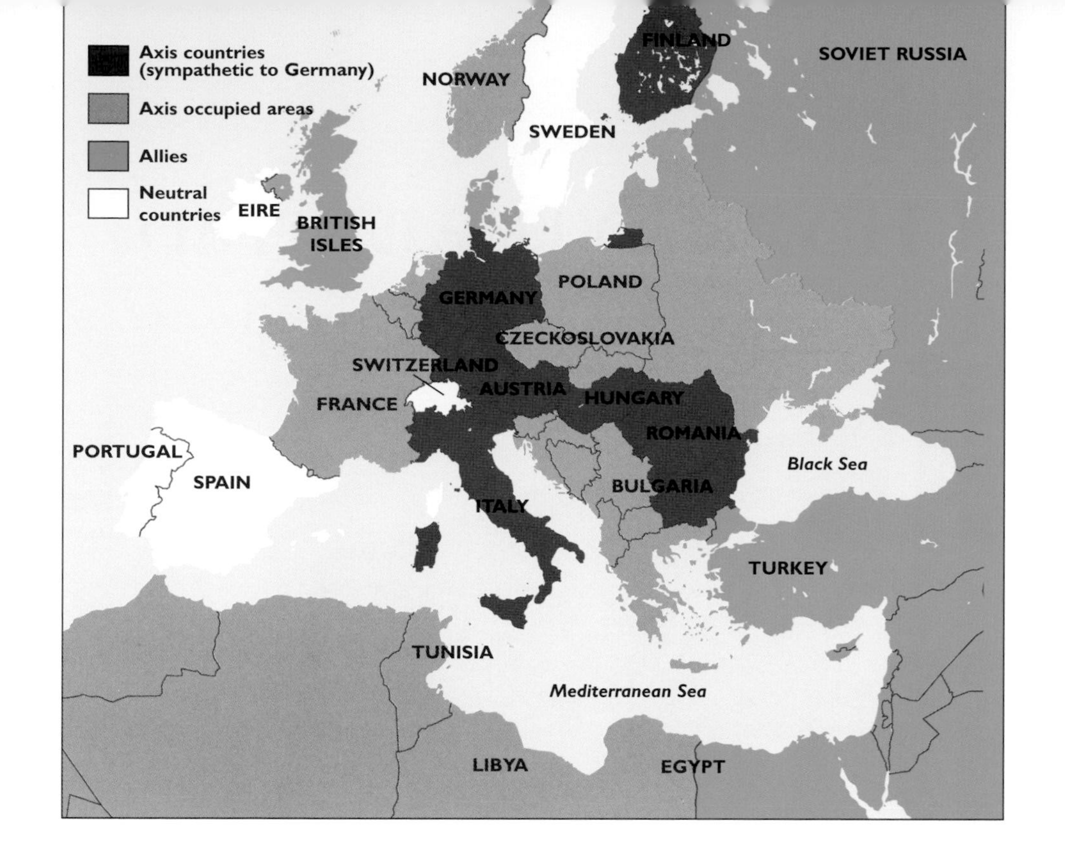

HOW STRONG WAS THE NAZI FIGHTING POWER?

FACT FILE

One of the greatest military operations ever carried out was the invasion of Europe by the Allied forces in 1944. Millions of troops were ferried across the English Channel and landed from floating harbors on the shores of France.

When the Germans realized that the British defenses were too strong for their aircraft, they tried to destroy British industry. They hoped to damage the morale of the British population by night-bombing their cities. The German *Luftwaffe*, which was considered to be far superior to the Royal Air Force (RAF), set out to bomb the British airfields and shoot down their aircraft. The *Luftwaffe* abandoned its attempts to defeat the RAF when they realized they were flying too far from home and ran short of fuel. As part of their policy to "purify" the German race, the Nazis had a plan to exterminate the Jews.

HOW DID THE UNITED NATIONS BEGIN?

The flag of the United Nations

During World War II, the Allied nations referred to themselves as the "United Nations." In 1942, they agreed that they would not make any separate peace agreements with Germany.

The Potsdam Conference, held in 1945, really laid the groundwork for the foundation of the United Nations. It was set up to prevent future conflict and to set out procedures for the prosecution of Nazi war criminals. Twenty-seven countries signed this first agreement. In 1945, after the war, the United Nations formally came into existence, with an initial membership of 50 countries.

The United Nations (UN) is led by a powerful Security Council, which can intervene in international disputes that might lead to conflict. Today, the UN is also involved in many economic aid programs around the world.

FACT FILE

Early in 1945, the Allied leaders met in Yalta, in the Crimea, to decide on the post-war shape of the world. Churchill, Roosevelt, and Stalin decided about how Germany was to be split up once the war was won.

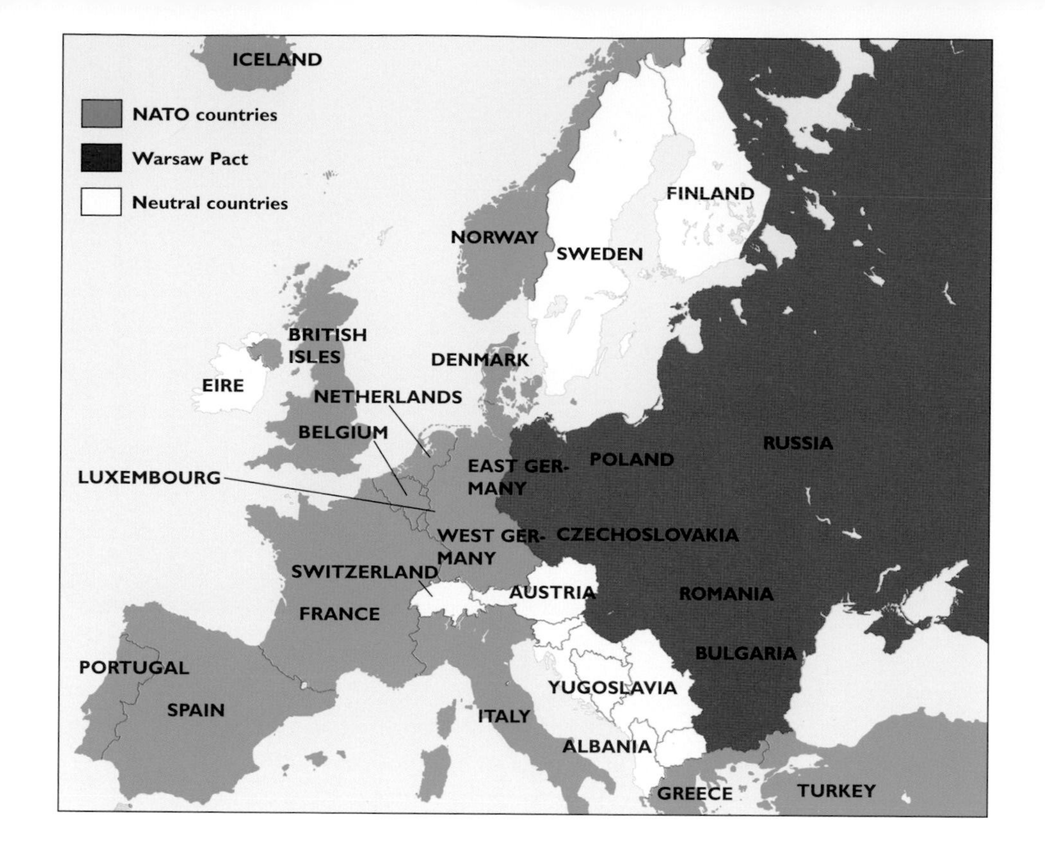

HOW DID THE COLD WAR AFFECT INTERNATIONAL RELATIONS?

A great of tension grew between the East and West after the war. Soviet forces suppressed attempts by Czechoslovakia and Hungary to obtain independence. However, nuclear war between the East and West did not occur. Instead, the Soviets provoked wars and political unrest in other countries, destabilizing governments of which they disapproved. The closest the world came to nuclear war was in 1962, when the Soviet Union moved missiles into Cuba, directly threatening the United States. The missiles were eventually removed, but only when the United States threatened retaliation.

FACT FILE

The Berlin Wall was built to stop people from escaping to the West. It finally came down in 1989 as the Soviet system collapsed.

WHAT?

CONTENTS

WHAT DID EARLY EXPLORERS USE FOR NAVIGATION?

An astrolabe

Early astronomers and navigators used instruments called *astrolabes* to measure the angles of celestial bodies above the horizon. An astrolabe is a metal disk mounted on a circular frame suspended vertically. The observer looks through the sights to line up a star and then measures its position against the marks on the frame. He can then use tables to work out his postion. The astrolabe remained in use from the time of the ancient Greeks until the seventeenth century, when it was replaced by more accurate instruments, such as the *sextant*.

People probably made rough maps even before they began to use written language some 5,500 years ago. Over the centuries, maps became more accurate as people explored the world and improved their ways of making maps. An early map of the world appeared in a 1482 edition of Ptolemy's eight-volume *Geography*, seen to the right.

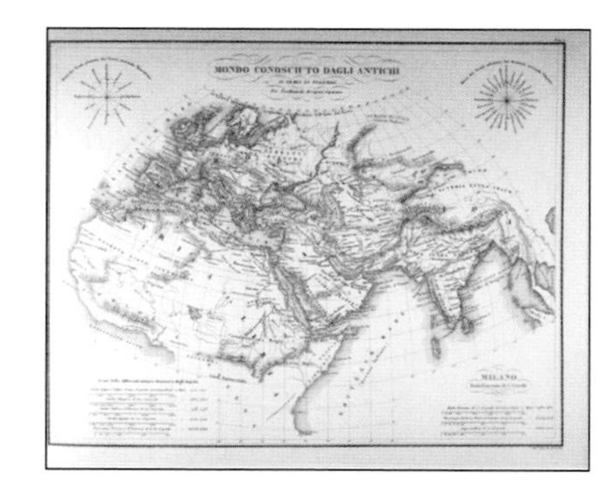

FACT FILE

Ferdinand Magellan was a Portuguese sea captain who commanded the first expedition to sail around the world. His voyage provided the first positive proof that the earth is round. Many scholars consider it the greatest navigational feat in history.

WHAT WAS DAILY LIFE LIKE IN ANCIENT GREECE?

Much of what we know about how the Greeks lived comes from pictures on vases. These pictures not only show wars and stories from mythology but also daily activities such as hunting, farming, and fishing. Greek homes were built around a central courtyard, cool and airy, where the family slaves prepared food on an open fire.

There was a small shrine to the household god. Many houses were made without windows in the outer walls. This design kept out the hot sun and thieves. People ate with their fingers, while lying on wooden couches. Slaves brought in the dishes of food, while a musician played on pipes or a lyre. Men and women wore a *chiton*, a cloth square draped over the body and fastened by a pin at the shoulder.

FACT FILE

This portrait of a Greek woman appeared on a fragment of pottery. Greek women spent most of their time around the home, organizing the household.

WHAT IS STONEHENGE?

Stonehenge on Salisbury Plain

More than 5,000 years ago, Europeans were building spectacular stone monuments. Many of these are still standing today, as mysterious relics belonging to a long-gone society. The huge stones they used are called *megaliths*, meaning "big stones." Some were set up by themselves, and others were arranged in groups or circles.

Stonehenge is a very famous Neolithic stone monument, which was built in several stages between 1800 and 1400 B.C. on Salisbury Plain, in England. No one really knows why it was built. It is set in a series of concentric rings of standing stones around an altar stone at the center. During the second stage, blue stones from the Preseli Mountains, in Wales, were hauled onto the site in an astonishing manner of organization and transport. The construction was highly accurate for the period. The standing stones measure up to 23 feet (7 m) high and weigh up to 50 tons (47 tonnes) each.

FACT FILE

Rock tombs, slab tombs, such as this dolmen, and stone circles and temples lie scattered across Europe, including on the island of Malta.

WHAT ARE HIEROGLYPHICS?

Egyptian picture-writing is known as *hieroglyphics*. This language is made up of about 750 signs, with pictures of people, animals, and objects. Until hieroglyphics was deciphered in modern times, it was not known that most of the pictures represented sounds and syllables, not whole words. Scribes used a quick form of writing, called *hieratic*. The Egyptians were also good at math, particularly geometry, which they used in architecture and surveying. They also drew up an accurate 12-month calendar of 365 days and used water clocks to measure time.

A chest from the tomb of Tutankhamen, an Egyptian king (c.1370–1352 B.C.)

FACT FILE

The Egyptian sun god Ra was often portrayed in picture form simply as a sun disk. He appeared in other forms, too, including as a cat, bird, and a lion.

WHAT WAS THE BYZANTINE EMPIRE?

FACT FILE

Byzantine traders used gold coins, called *bezants*. These coins have been found across Asia as far as China and as far west as Britain.

The Roman empire split in two in 395 A.D. After the collapse of the western half in 476 A.D., the eastern part survived. Its capital was called Byzantium, now Istanbul, in Turkey, a city founded by the Greeks. The Roman emperor Constantine gave the city of Byzantium a new name, Constantinople. The Byzantine Empire comprised Turkey, the Balkans, parts of Spain and North Africa, Egypt, and the western coasts of the Mediterranean. The Empire was at its height under the rule of the sixth-century emperor Justinian and his influential wife, Theodora. Through war and diplomacy, Justinian made Byzantium the greatest power in the eastern Mediterranean.

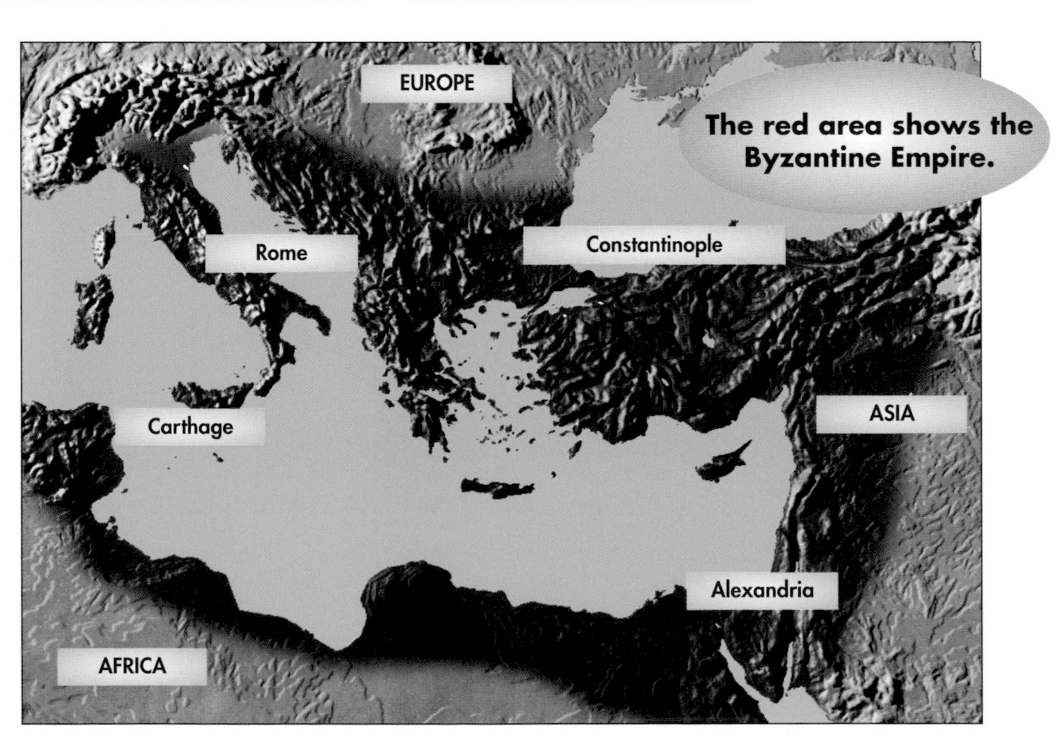

The red area shows the Byzantine Empire.

WHAT WAS EARLY MONASTERY LIFE LIKE?

In the 500s A.D., an Italian named Benedict of Nursia drew up a set of rules for monks, those people who lived in monasteries. All monks must be poor, unmarried, and obedient. Monks wore simple robes, shaved their heads, and shared all their daily tasks.

Monasteries were for men only. Religious women joined orders of their own and became nuns. Each monastery was led by an abbot, some of whom had as much power as any nobleman, controlling farms, trades, and even private armies.

Monks grew their own food, reared farm animals, baked bread, and brewed beer. They made their own clothes and furniture, and built their own churches. They also looked after the sick. Part of their time was spent teaching young boys, who would in time become monks themselves.

FACT FILE

The monastery at Mont Saint-Michel in France was built by Benedictine monks in 966 A.D. It stands on a tiny island in Normandy, linked by a causeway to the French mainland.

What is Sutton Hoo?

The most powerful ruler among the English kings was called as *bretwalda*, or "supreme king."

The Sutton Hoo ship burial site in Suffolk, England, was discovered in 1939 A.D. It is almost certainly the monument to King Redwald of East Anglia, who was bretwalda in the 620s A.D. 620s, and who died in 627 A.D.

Artefacts unearthed by archaeologists at the Sutton Hoo site included a gold belt, a sword, and a shield. There were also several items of jewelery. Most important were a scepter and standard, which must have belonged to the King Redwald. The iron helmet to the right was another one of the treasures unearthed at Sutton Hoo.

FACT FILE

The Scots' leader, Kenneth MacAlpin, was the first king to rule the land we now call Scotland. Raiders from the north, the Picts and Scots, attacked northern England once the Roman army were no longer around to protect the Roman Britons of England.

WHAT WERE THE CRUSADES?

FACT FILE

Richard I of England and Philip II of France led the armies of the Third Crusade, setting sail for the Holy Land in 1189.

The Byzantine emperor, a Christian monarch who lived in Constantinople, needed help. He turned to the pope, who in 1095 called for all Christians to start a holy war against the Seljuk Turks.

Thousands rushed to join the Crusader armies. They crossed into Palestine and recaptured the key cities of Nicaea and Antioch. Jerusalem fell in 1099 after a desperate siege lasting six weeks. The Crusaders took terrible revenge by slaughtering thousands of Muslims. There were to be three more crusades: one in 1147–48, another in 1189–92, and finally the Children's Crusade in 1212. Some 50,000 children set off from France and Germany for the Holy Land. Many died on the journey, while many more were captured and sold as slaves in Africa.

WHAT WAS THE MAGNA CARTA?

The youngest son of Henry II, John, inherited the throne of England from his brother Richard, as well as the Plantagenet dominions of France, which he had lost to the French by 1204. King John's failure to recapture these territories, his dispute with Rome over the Pope's choice of a new Archbishop of Canterbury, and a high level of taxation had the English nobility up in arms against him.

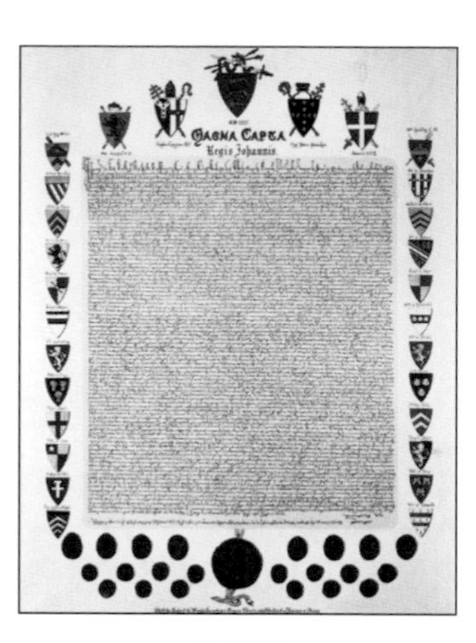

Magna Carta

In 1215, they forced King John to agree to the Magna Carta, guaranteeing their rights in relation to those of the crown. It was intended to protect the rights of nobles and to make sure that no one was imprisoned without a fair trial. Copies of this document, which tried to put an end to the king's abuse of his power, were distributed across all of England. This led to civil war, which ended only with John's death in 1216.

Despite these disasters, it is now known that John was a much better king than history had portrayed him.

FACT FILE

The Magna Carta was a document signed by King John in 1215, guaranteeing feudal rights to the barons. After his death, the barons renegotiated the charter with his son and it became part of English law.

WHAT WAS THE BLACK DEATH?

The bubonic plague, or "Black Death," was a deadly disease that brought death to most parts of Asia, North Africa, and Europe. The first outbreak was recorded in 1331, in China. The plague started as a bloody swelling in the armpit or groin and quickly invaded the whole body. It was highly contagious and killed millions of people. The infection probably began on the grassy plains of Asia. It was carried by fleas that lived in the fur of the black rat. The rats lived close to human beings and thus the disease spread rapidly. Corpses were left out in the road for people to collect, making the disease spread even further.

FACT FILE

Medieval paintings often depicted death as a skeleton, dancing and leading victims to their end. The epidemic killed at least 25,000,000 people in Europe and the Near East.

WHAT DO WE KNOW ABOUT THE EARLY HISTORY OF AFRICA?

FACT FILE

A view showing what the Great Enclosure may have looked like inside the city of Great Zimbabwe.

We know very little about the early history of Africa. There must have been great civilizations there, but very few of them developed writing or left any records. Some civilizations built fine communities, such as the east coast port of Kilwa or the mysterious stone complex of Great Zimbabwe. After about 700 A.D., Muslims from the Near East began to take over many coastal regions and trade routes. One of the wealthiest of the medieval African empires was Mali. Starting in 1240, its Islamic rulers built up a kingdom that stretched over 1800 mi. (1,600 km) over West Africa. Much of the land was desert, but Mali grew rich from gold.

Timbuktu in Mali. Founded in the late 11th century

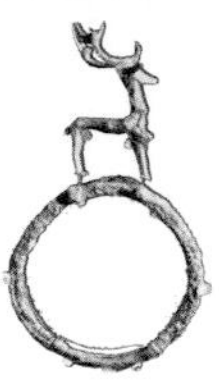

By 1550, Spain ruled most of Central and South America and the West Indies. Fleets of Spanish galleons carried gold and silver and plundered treasures across the Atlantic to Europe.

WHAT WAS THE NEW WORLD?

From 1492 on, European explorers sailed across the Atlantic to what they called the New World of North, Central, and South America. There, they discovered a treasure trove of gold and silver. They also discovered foods that grew only in the New World, such as sweet corn, potatoes, and plants that could be made into medicines.

The people that settled in the New World were traders, rather than soldiers. Their first contact with the people already living there was friendly. The Native Americans showed the newcomers how to hunt, fish, and farm in a land of plenty. In return, they were given objects such as knives, needles, fish hooks, and cloth.

FACT FILE

This depicts a modern replica of the *Mayflower*, the ship in which the first Pilgrims set sail from England, in 1620.

WHAT WAS THE INDUSTRIAL REVOLUTION?

FACT FILE

Raw cotton, grown mainly in the United States, was very difficult and slow to clean. Whitney's cotton gin was a simple machine that brushed out the seeds from the cotton.

One of the biggest changes in the history of the world, the Industrial Revolution, started in Britain in the late eighteenth century. Britain was the first home of new machines, new types of materials, and new ways of making power. This was the age of coal and iron, of electricity and gas, of railways and factories. These factories created millions of new jobs, so people began to leave the countryside to work in the towns. Houses and factories had to be built for them. By 1850, over 60 percent of British workers lived in towns. Factory workers led hard lives, often working 14 hours a day, 6 days a week.

Ironworks at Coalbrookdale in Shropshire, England

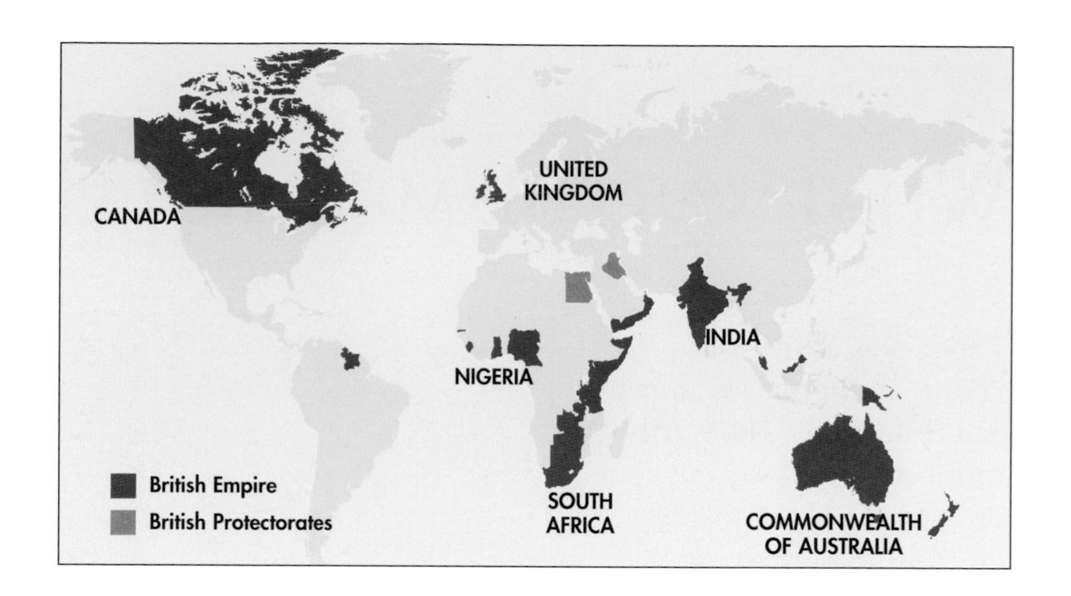

WHAT WAS THE EXTENT OF BRITAIN'S COLONIES IN THE EIGHTEENTH CENTURY?

Britain had started her collection of overseas colonies during the reign of Elizabeth I. By 1602, both England and the Netherlands had founded an East India Company on the Indian coast to trade with the Far East.

The first settlements in North America took root and flourished in early Stuart times. In 1661, Britain gained her first African foothold, seizing James Island on the Gambia River. By the middle of the 1700s, these scattered colonies had begun to grow into a powerful and profitable empire. By the 1750s, the British navy ruled the seas. By 1763, Britain had taken over most of France's territory in North America. The map above shows the extent of its empire in 1821.

FACT FILE

British General James Wolfe brought French power in North America to an end. Wolfe's troops attacked and seized the city of Quebec. He died before the battle of Quebec ended.

WHAT WAS THE MEIJI RULE?

The 1860s was a time of uncertainty and political unrest in Japan. Finally, in 1868, the situation became so serious that Emperor Mutsuhito took control from the last shogun. Mutsuhito became known as the Meiji emperor, and the event is called the *Meiji restoration*.

Under the emperor's authority, Japan embarked on a modernization program. In 1872, a group of Japanese politicians went on a tour of Europe and North America to learn more about industry, education, and the ways of life in the West. As a result, factories were built in Japan and the country started to change from an agricultural to an industrialized nation. This also included the establishment of a national railway system. During the period of Meiji rule, education was introduced for all Japanese people. The Meiji emperor also gave farmers ownership of their lands and changed Japan's army and navy into modern military forces.

FACT FILE

During the Meiji period, Japan wanted to extend its territories. In 1894–95 its forces crushed the Chinese navy and gained control of Taiwan. Here you can see a Chinese ship sinking during the battle of Yalu, in 1894.

WHAT WAS HOME RULE?

In 1870, a movement calling for Home Rule was founded in Ireland. Supporters of Home Rule wanted a separate parliament to deal with Irish affairs in Dublin. Although the British government was forced to introduce many reforms, two bills to introduce Home Rule were defeated in parliament in the 1880s and 1890s. William Gladstone was Prime Minister of Britain four times during the reign of Queen Victoria. He believed that the Irish should run their own affairs and was a staunch supporter of Home Rule, but he failed to get his Home Rule Bill approved by parliament.

William Gladstone

During World War I, the issue of Home Rule continued to cause conflict in Ireland. The third Home Rule Bill had been passed by the British parliament in 1914, but the outbreak of war in the same year delayed its start. Irish protestants, however, were bitterly opposed to Home Rule. They were in the majority in the northern province of Ulster, and believed that they would be treated unfairly by a Dublin parliament. They formed the Ulster Volunteer Force to protect themselves if Home Rule was introduced.

The Irish flag

FACT FILE

Irish politician Charles Parnell addresses an audience in support of Home Rule. He became leader of the Home Rule Party in the British parliament and fought tirelessly for his beliefs.

The Suez Canal

WHAT IS THE SUEZ CANAL?

FACT FILE

Queen Victoria was on the throne when the Suez Canal was begun and when it opened. During her reign, which lasted 63 years, Britain's empire expanded greatly.

The concept of a canal linking the Mediterranean to the Red Sea dates back to ancient times. It was Napoleon's engineers who, around 1800 A.D., revived the idea of a shorter route to India via the Suez Canal. It was not until 1859 that Egyptian workers started working on the construction of the Canal by using slave labor. The project was completed around 1867.

Although Britain had played no part in building the Suez Canal in Egypt, it benefited greatly when it opened. The new 120 mi. long (190 km) waterway shortened the route from Britain to India by approximately 6,000 mi. (9,700 km), thereby extending their ability to trade.

WHAT WAS "CUSTER'S LAST STAND"?

The Battle at Little Big Horn

George Armstrong Custer first came to be known as a cavalry officer during the Civil War (1861–1865). In 1866, he led the 7th Cavalry against the Native Americans of the Great Plains. In 1874, he led an expedition that discovered gold in the Black Hills of the Dakota Territory and began the Gold Rush. The hills were sacred to the Cheyenne and Sioux Indians, and relations between these Indians and the white invaders deteriorated. In 1876, Custer led the 7th Cavalry against an alliance of Cheyenne and Sioux warriors. He went into battle against thousands of warriors in the valley of the Little Big Horn River. He and his main unit of 250 soldiers were all killed in what became known as "Custer's Last Stand."

FACT FILE

Bold pioneers made their way in long trains of covered wagons, drawn by the stories of gold in the hills. However, very few actually made their fortunes.

WHAT WAS STEPHENSON'S ROCKET?

FACT FILE

Another important invention took place in 1840, when the American inventor Samuel F. B. Morse launched a code based on dots, dashes, and spaces. Known as the Morse code, it speeded up the sending of messages through the telegraph.

Modern rail travel owes its existence to the great engineer George Stephenson. While working as a mechanic in a coal mine, he educated himself at night school. By 1812, he was a chief mechanic and in 1814, he built his first locomotive, the *Blucher*.

This locomotive propelled itself at 4 mi. (6 km) per hour and could pull eight wagons loaded with coal. Stephenson refined the steam engine until he built the first practical steam locomotive, the *Rocket*, in 1829. It could travel at an amazing 36 mi. (58 km) per hour.

George Stephenson

WHAT WAS THE WOMEN'S MOVEMENT?

FACT FILE

In Britain, the suffragette campaigners often went on hunger strikes when imprisoned for their actions. The authorities did not want them to die and thereby arouse public sympathy, so they fed the women by force.

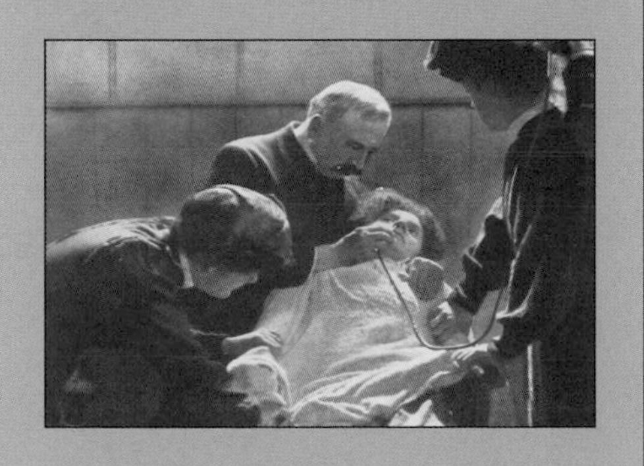

The women's movement had its roots in the late eighteenth and early nineteenth centuries. The American and French revolutions promoted ideas of "equality" and "liberty," yet women could not vote and had limited access to education.

In 1792, a British writer named Mary Wollstonecraft published a book called *A Vindication of the Rights of Women*, which set forth her belief in equal rights for men and women. This idea took a firm hold during the 1800s, and many women started to campaign for reform. The suffragettes, those who advocated rights for women, engaged in many different forms of protest, including chaining themselves to railings outside the residence of the British Prime Minister.

WHAT WERE NINETEENTH-CENTURY SLUMS LIKE?

The events of the Industrial Revolution brought great changes to towns and cities. People needed to live close to their workplace, so large numbers of houses were built to accommodate this new class of industrial worker. The speed with which many towns and cities expanded led to problems with overcrowding, and dirty and unsanitary housing. Many workers were forced to live in slum conditions. Worse, the new factories created pollution that often contaminated both the water supply and the air. Early industrial cities were disease-ridden places with very high death rates.

FACT FILE

Life in the industrial centers revolved around the mines, mills, and factories where people worked.

Pollution from the new factories

WHAT WAS THE GREAT DEPRESSION?

A disastrous stock market crash in 1929 in the United States left many people penniless overnight. The effects of the Wall Street Crash were felt all over the world. Many countries in Europe were hard hit because they had borrowed money from the United States at the end of World War I. Throughout the 1930s, unemployment soared and trade slumped in a period known as the Great Depression.

During the worst years of the Depression, many people were forced to rely on charity and government handouts for their most basic needs. In 1932, Franklin D. Roosevelt was elected President. His New Deal aimed to create jobs and to protect people's savings by regulating banks more closely.

FACT FILE

This is the Stock Exchange in Wall Street at the time of its collapse. It depicts brokers spilling out of the building onto the streets of New York City.

WHAT WAS THE TREATY OF VERSAILLES?

The signing of the Treaty of Versailles

FACT FILE

The signing of the Treaty of Versailles on June 28, 1919, in Paris, was the fifth anniversary of the shooting of Archduke Ferdinand in Sarajevo.

The Treaty of Versailles was a peace document signed at the end of World War I by the Allied and Associated Powers and by Germany. It took place in the Hall of Mirrors at the Palace of Versailles, France, on June 28, 1919. It was not enforced until January 10, 1920.

The treaty was drafted during the Paris Peace Conference in the spring of 1919, which was dominated by the national leaders known as the Big Four. These men were David Lloyd George of Britain, Georges Clemenceau of France, Woodrow Wilson of the United States, and Vittorio Orlando of Italy. They wanted to make sure that Germany would never again pose a military threat. The treaty contained a number of stipulations to guarantee this.

WHAT WAS THE EASTER RISING?

FACT FILE

The British Prime Minister, David Lloyd George, proposed that Ireland would stay under British control, but the Irish Free State would become a British dominion.

During World War I, the issue of Home Rule continued to cause conflict in Ireland. When war actually broke out in 1914, most Irish Volunteers supported Britain in its fight against the Central Powers. However, a breakaway group formed the Irish Republican Brotherhood, later known as the Irish Republican Army, or IRA. On Easter Monday, 1916, protesters belonging to this and other nationalist movements seized buildings in Dublin and proclaimed Ireland a republic. This rebellion became known as the Easter Rising.

Easter Monday, 1916

WHAT WAS THE BATTLE OF BRITAIN?

During World War II, the Allied forces of Britain and France became trapped by the rapid German invasion. In June 1940, the French signed a truce with Germany, and Britain stood alone against the Germans.

Italy joined the war, siding with the Germans. In June 1940, Hitler made plans to invade Britain. However, he first needed to gain control of the skies. The Battle of Britain began in July 1940 between the German airforce, the *Luftwaffe*, and Britain's Royal Air Force (RAF). By May 1941, the RAF had gained the upper hand, and Hitler stopped the bombing.

FACT FILE

Allied troops wait on a beach at Dunkirk, in northern France, in June 1940. A rescue fleet of naval ships, fishing boats, yachts, and ferries sailed across the English Channel from England to carry them back to safety. In all, 300,000 soldiers were rescued.

WHAT WAS THE HOLOCAUST?

Jews held in a concentration camp

In the early 1930s, the Nazi party rose to power in Germany, led by Adolf Hitler. He set up a secret police force, banned opposing political parties, and started to persecute minority groups in the German population, such as gypsies and Jews.

During World War II, concentration camps such as Belsen and Auschwitz were set up by the Nazis. Millions of Jews were imprisoned and murdered in these camps because Hitler believed they were responsible for the downfall of Germany. An estimated 6,000,000 Jews died in these camps during World War II, an event known as the *Holocaust*.

FACT FILE

The official flag of the United Nations consists of a map of the world circled by two olive branches. The olive branches are a symbol of peace.

WHAT WAS THE BLITZKRIEG?

World War II was very different to the first international conflict, World War I. Trench warfare, which had claimed so many lives, was now an outdated concept. When Adolf Hitler invaded Poland in September 1939, he unleashed a new and frightening brand of warfare into the world, called *Blitzkrieg*, or "lightning war."

The key to the success of Blitzkrieg was its use of tanks in very large numbers and innovative style. The tanks charged ahead independently of the troops and wreaked havoc among the defenders. Bursting through defensive lines, they created confusion and smashed supply lines.

FACT FILE

World War II had deadly new weaponry as well. The introduction of machine guns changed the way the armies fought from the trenches. They could now easily wipe out large numbers of attacking soldiers.

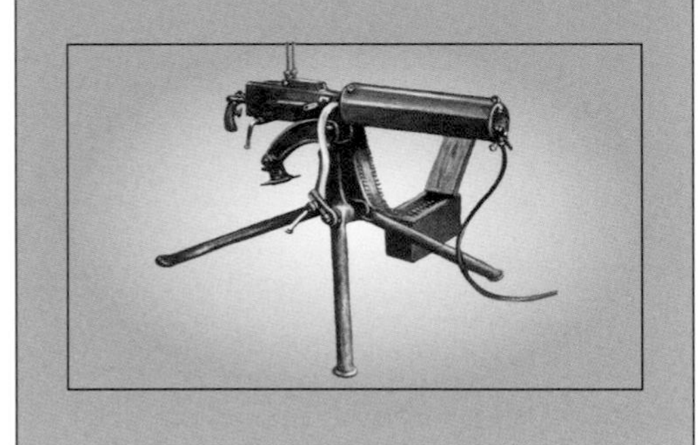

Tanks used during Blitzkrieg

WHAT IS COMMUNISM?

FACT FILE

Chairman Mao and his supporters accused many people of failing to follow communist ideals. Students and young people formed groups of "Red Guards" to support Mao.

Communism is a system of political and economic organization in which property is owned by the state and all citizens share the common wealth. After years of civil war, much of China was in ruins. Mao Zedong set about reforming the country according to communist ideals. Land was seized from landowners and divided up among the peasants. In Mao's Five-Year Plan (1953–1957) new roads and railways were built, industry grew, and health and education improved. Mao printed the ideals of his communist state in what became known as Mao's *Little Red Book*, which was read by millions of Chinese.

WHAT WAS THE CUBAN MISSILE CRISIS?

In 1949, the Western Allies formed the North Atlantic Treaty Organization (NATO) for defense against the communist presence in Europe. In that same year, the Union of Soviet Socialist Republic (USSR) exploded its first atomic bomb. With both superpowers holding nuclear weapons, fear and mistrust between the two sides increased. The Soviets constructed a wall across Berlin in 1961, separating East from West in the city. In 1962, the Cuban crisis erupted when the United States discovered that the USSR was building missile sites on the island of Cuba, in the Caribbean. These sites were within range to launch an attack by nuclear weapons on American cities. The two superpowers came to the brink of war before the USSR agreed to withdraw its weapons.

Although the two superpowers never became involved in direct warfare, both sides became involved in wars elsewhere in the world. The United States fought communism and the USSR helped communist fighters.

FACT FILE

John Fitzgerald Kennedy was President from 1961 until he was assassinated in 1963. During his presidency, the Berlin Wall was built, dividing the city in two and stopping East Germans escaping communist rule.

WHAT WAS THE ATLANTIC CHARTER?

At the height of World War II, in August 1941, the president of the United States, Franklin D. Roosevelt, and the British Prime Minister, Winston Churchill, met for a shipboard conference off the coast of Newfoundland. They signed a declaration, known as The Atlantic Charter, which expressed the post-war aims of these two countries. They promised to promote peace, stability, and democracy and to disarm aggressor nations. Two short excerpts from the Charter follows:

"... First, their countries seek no aggrandizement, territorial or other; Second, they desire to see no territorial changes that do not accord with the freely expressed wishes of the peoples concerned ... Eighth, they believe that all the nations of the world, for realistic as well as spiritual reasons, must come to the abandonment of the use of force ..."

FACT FILE

Representatives from 26 countries signed a document known as the Declaration of United Nations on January 1, 1942. Another 21 countries later signed the Declaration.

WHEN?

CONTENTS

WHEN WAS THE STONE AGE?

The Stone Age occurred about 100,000 to 35,000 years ago. The people who lived during this time in Europe are known as *Neanderthal people*. They lived in caves, used fire, and hunted animals using stone tools and wooden spears.

Historians call this period of prehistory the *Stone Age* because stone was the most important material used by the first toolmakers. Their early stone-crafting techniques show surprising skill. They chipped or flaked off bits of stone to make shaped tools, including hand axes and knives. Both the hand axe and scraper were usually made from flint. Spear heads were often shaped from wood or deer antlers.

Stone Age hunters killed deer and other animals with spears, bows, and stones, often ambushing them on the move. Although they were not as fast as the animals they hunted, they made up for it by using teamwork and accuracy with their weapons.

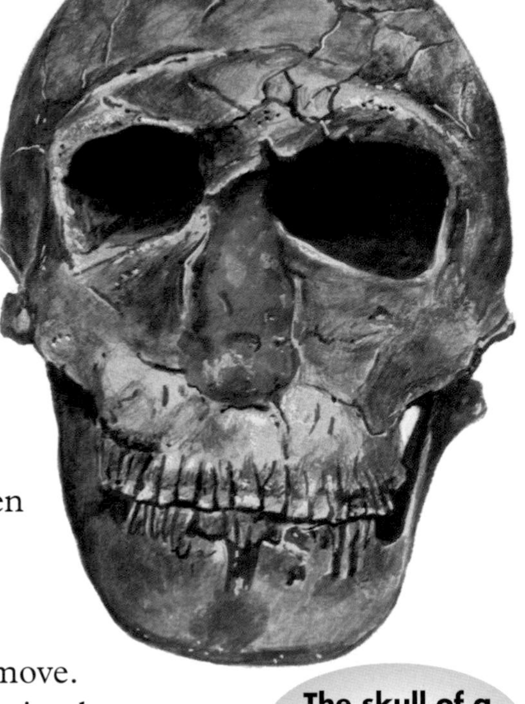

The skull of a Neanderthal man

Spear head

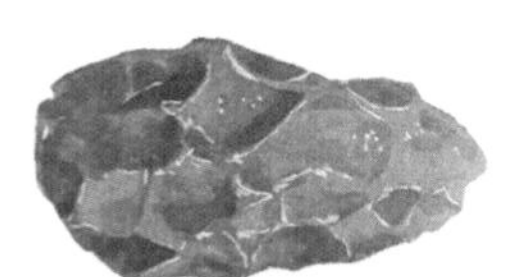

Scraper

Hand ax

FACT FILE

Stone Age people hunted with bows, spears, and flint axes. In America, groups of hunters drove to extinction large grazing animals, such as mastodons and bison.

WHEN WAS BABYLON FOUNDED?

After the fall the city of Ur in 2000 B.C., many cities of Mesopotamia were ruled by the Amorites, whose two strongholds were the cities of Isin and Larsa. In 1763 B.C., Larsa fell to a great army led by Hammurabi (1792–1750 B.C.). The new ruler gave the kingdoms of Sumer and Akkad a new name, *Babylonia*.

The Ishtar Gate, Babylon

The city of Babylon had magnificent temples and palaces. People entered the city through eight great bronze gates. The most magnificent of these was the Ishtar Gate, which was decorated with shiny, patterned bricks in patterns and pictures of lions, bulls, and dragons. Babylon's winding, narrow streets were lined with houses. Most had a courtyard with rooms around it. The city walls had gates, around which traders held markets. Traders and merchants traveled from as far as Syria, Assyria, and the kingdoms of the Persian Gulf.

The Babylonians produced written records by carving picture symbols onto clay tablets. The tablets carried information about astronomy, mathematics, legal records, business matters, and religious texts.

FACT FILE

The ancient Babylonians were the first people to study the stars, some time before 2000 B.C. They knew of five planets: Jupiter, Mars, Mercury, Saturn, and Venus.

WHEN WAS THE START OF SAXON BRITAIN?

FACT FILE

Treasures found in a burial site at Sutton Hoo, Suffolk, included a gold belt, a sword and shield, an iron helmet, and several jewels.

In the late 300s A.D., the Roman army was struggling to fight off waves of barbarian invasions. Troops in distant outposts, such as the British Isles, were needed to defend the empire, and by 410 A.D., the last Roman soldiers had left England for mainland Europe. Without the Roman army to protect them, the Roman Britons of England were unable to prevent invaders from taking over the land they wanted. The newcomers were a mixture of people–Angles, Saxons, Jutes, Frisians–who became known as the *English*. The invaders came to England to find farmland. They were well armed, tough, and drove away many Britons, who moved into western England.

Saxon farmers

Ships lie beside a Viking town

WHEN DID THE VIKINGS RAID EUROPE?

The Vikings were a group of people who came from Scandinavia (Norway, Denmark, and Sweden). Their homelands offered little spare farmland for a growing population. So, many Vikings went abroad in search of new land. The Vikings were farmers but also were fierce warriors. Their first impact on western Europe was a violent one. They set sail across the North Sea in the late 700s A.D., raiding the coasts of Britain and mainland Europe. They raided churches and towns, carrying off loot and slaves. Their raids created panic, and rulers tried to buy off the invaders with gold. This, however, only encouraged the Vikings to come back for more.

FACT FILE

Decorative brooches were used by both Viking men and women to hold their outer clothing in place.

When was the Hundred Years' War?

The 14th century was filled with wars. The longest and most exhausting of these wars was between England and France. It lasted, on and off, until the middle of the 1400s. It is known as the Hundred Years' War. This war actually spanned from 1337 until 1453. By 1453, the French, inspired by Joan of Arc, had driven the English from Maine, Gascony, and Normandy. The war was finally won by the French. The conflict was a very complicated one. The Plantagenet king of England ruled a large part of France, while the rest belonged to the king of France. Both kings wanted to be the sole ruler of a united country. There were also other reasons for the war. For example, the French supported the Scots in their struggle against England. Also, the English claimed the throne of France when Charles IV died in 1328 and left no heirs.

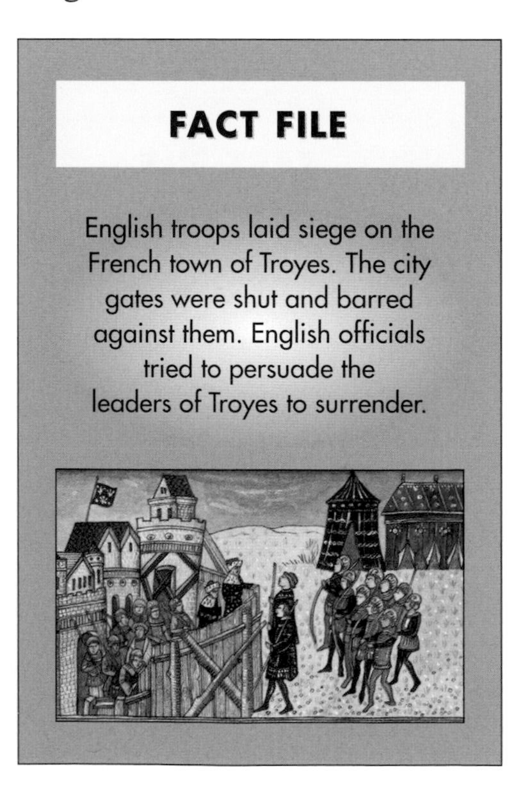

FACT FILE

English troops laid siege on the French town of Troyes. The city gates were shut and barred against them. English officials tried to persuade the leaders of Troyes to surrender.

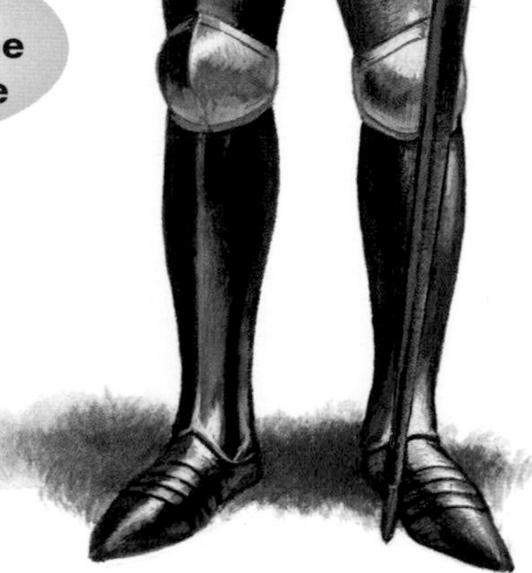

Edward, known as the Black Prince

WHEN DID THE GREAT NATIONS OF EUROPE EMERGE?

After about 1450, the great nations of Europe began to emerge. For most of their history, these countries had consisted of small warring states, or they had been invaded by powerful neighbors. Now, things were quickly changing.

The connection between France and England was broken at last. Spain and Portugal grew stable enough to develop as great seagoing empires. Germany (part of the Holy Roman Empire) had strong leaders from the Habsburg dynasty. The marriage of King Ferdinand and Queen Isabella of Spain in 1492 helped to unite the two strong Christian kingdoms of Aragon and Castile. Ferdinand and Isabella completed the great "reconquest" of Spain from Muslim control, which had begun over 400 years earlier.

FACT FILE

Unlike Spain, Italy remained a divided country, split up into states ruled by different powers. In the north were the wealthy city-states, such as Florence, Milan, and Urbino. The crest below belonged to the Sforza family, who ruled over Milan.

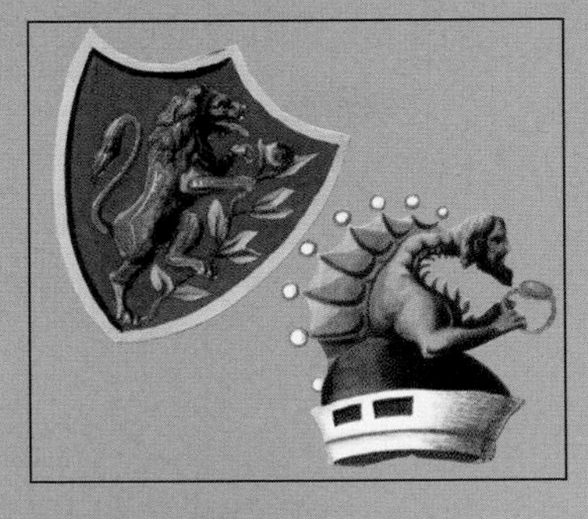

King Ferdinand and Queen Isabella

WHEN WAS THE THIRTY YEARS' WAR?

The last large religious war began in Germany in 1618 and continued until 1648. This very messy conflict became known as the Thirty Years' War.

The war started in a dramatic way. Protestants in Bohemia (which is now part of the Czech Republic) were angry with their new king, Ferdinand. He was a member of the powerful Spanish Habsburg family and wanted to restore Bohemia to the Catholic faith. The Protestants banded together to throw some Catholic officials from an upstairs window in the Prague Castle. The incident sparked a civil war in Bohemia. In 1619, the rebels expelled Ferdinand and chose a new Protestant king, Frederick.

FACT FILE

Protestants threw Catholic officials out of a window in the Prague Castle. It became known as the "Defenestration of Prague."

WHEN WAS THE CIVIL WAR IN BRITAIN?

In 1603, Britain had a new king, James I. He was the first of the Stuart monarchs and ruled not only England and Wales, but also Scotland. James strongly believed that God had given kings their right to govern. He thought no one could question this authority. James's arrogant views and conduct made him unpopular with his subjects. His son, Charles I, followed him to the throne in 1625. He was even less popular. Soon, Britain was split by civil war. Charles wanted to rule without consulting parliament, but he was faced with enormous rebellion. Enraged by this, Charles tried to arrest five members of parliament for treason. The action made him hated even more, and he was forced to flee to London. By August 1642, he had declared war on the parliamentary supporters, known as *Roundheads*.

FACT FILE

A Roundhead helmet. Oliver Cromwell reorganized the Roundhead forces into a professional force known as the "New Model Army."

In 1644, a combined force of Scots and Roundheads defeated Charles and his Royalist forces at the battle of Marston Moor in Yorkshire.

WHEN WAS THE SLAVE TRADE ABOLISHED IN AFRICA?

During the 1700s, the slave trade transported thousands of Africans across the Atlantic Ocean and forced them to work as slaves on plantations in America. This trade brought huge wealth to the shipbuilders, shipowners, merchants, and traders who ran it.

Many people began to condemn the slave trade and fought for it to be abolished. The slave trade ended in the British Empire in 1807. It was finally abolished within the empire in 1833. Slavery continued elsewhere, however. It did not come to an end in the United States until after the Civil War in 1865. It continued in Brazil until 1889.

In 1788, an association was formed in London to encourage British exploration and trade in Africa. Many British explorers set out to explore Africa along its rivers. Probably the most famous of all the expeditions was led by David Livingstone, who set out to look for the source of the Nile River.

David Livingstone

FACT FILE

The abolitionist movement was strongest in England and the U.S.A. Many people joined the struggle to end slavery.

A typical colonist's hat

WHEN WERE THE OPIUM WARS?

The Manchus ruled China for more than 250 years, from 1644 to 1912. This time is referred to as the Qing dynasty. In the early 1800s, British merchants started to trade opium illegally from India to China. Despite the fact that the addictive dangers of opium were well known, the British government backed the merchants. They wanted to force China to accept more open trade.

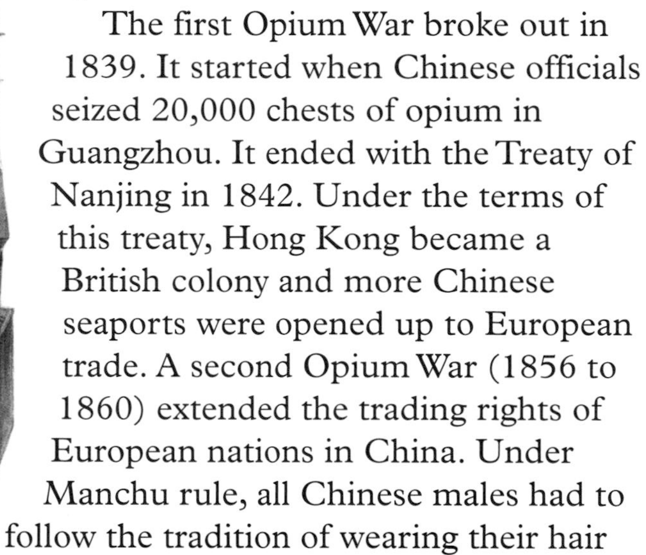

The first Opium War broke out in 1839. It started when Chinese officials seized 20,000 chests of opium in Guangzhou. It ended with the Treaty of Nanjing in 1842. Under the terms of this treaty, Hong Kong became a British colony and more Chinese seaports were opened up to European trade. A second Opium War (1856 to 1860) extended the trading rights of European nations in China. Under Manchu rule, all Chinese males had to follow the tradition of wearing their hair in a pigtail. This was seen as a sign of loyalty to the Qing dynasty.

FACT FILE

This picture shows the skyline of modern Hong Kong. The island of Hong Kong came under British control in 1842, and Britain later gained part of the nearby Kowloon Peninsula. Control of Hong Kong passed back to the Chinese government in 1997.

When was the Russian Revolution?

The last Russian tsar, Nicholas II, ruled from 1894 until his abdication in 1917. In the early years of his reign, there was increasing discontent among common Russians. Many people, including the Bolshevik leader Vladimir Illyich Lenin, followed the teachings of Karl Marx, the founder of communism. In 1905, this discontent boiled over when troops fired on thousands of striking workers outside the tsar's Winter Palace in St Petersburg. The rebellion was quickly stopped, but hundreds of workers were killed and wounded.

In early 1917, riots broke out again. This time, the troops supported the rioters. Nicholas II abdicated, and a provisional government was put in place.

FACT FILE

Imprisoned by the Bolsheviks in 1917, Nicholas II and his family were probably killed the following year.

WHEN DID SETTLERS FIRST ARRIVE IN JAPAN?

People from mainland Asia settled on the islands of Japan around 7000 B.C. The original inhabitants may have been the Ainu, about 15,000 of whom still live in Japan. The early Japanese lived by hunting and fishing. Farming began around 1,000 to 500 B.C., when the Japanese learned to grow rice, a skill brought over from China. They also began to make metal tools and pottery. The site in Tokyo where pottery was first found gives this period of history its name–Yayoi.

The Yayoi farmers dug ditches to irrigate their rice fields. They built thatched homes and storehouses on stilts for their rice crop. Farmers lived together in villages, and each village was led by a chief who was often a woman shaman, or magician. The women shamans of Japan were extremely powerful figures.

FACT FILE

During Japan's Yayoi period, the dead were often buried inside stone tombs, like the one shown here.

When did Wall Street Crash?

In the late 1920s, the price of shares on the New York Stock Exchange increased rapidly. More and more people bought stocks and shares. They hoped to sell them again when their price had gone up and make a large profit. When prices dropped in October of 1929, people rushed to sell their stocks and shares before it was too late, but the prices fell even further. This event is known as the Wall Street Crash. Thousands of people lost all of their money. Many businesses and banks shut down, and unemployment soared.

FACT FILE

During the worst years of the Depression, many people were forced to rely on charity and government hand-outs for their most basic needs. In 1932, Franklin D. Roosevelt was elected president. His "New Deal" aimed to create jobs and to protect people's savings by regulating banks more closely.

The Stock Exchange at the time of the collapse

WHEN WAS THE RISE OF FASCISM IN EUROPE?

Many people hoped that World War I was the "war to end all wars." However, during the 1920s and 1930s, there were a lot of political changes going on in many countries. In 1922, these changes led to the growth of the fascist movement. The word *fascism* means *a bundle of branches*. Fascism promised strong leadership and to restore the economy and pride. This was a very powerful message in the years of the Great Depression. Many people in Europe supported the fascist parties.

Italy was the first country to have a fascist ruler. In 1922, Benito Mussolini marched to Rome and demanded that the Italian king, Victor Emmanuel III, make him Prime Minister.

FACT FILE

Sir Oswald Mosley knew Adolf Hitler through his wife, Diana Mitford. Mosley was violently opposed to postwar "nonwhite" immigration.

WHEN WAS THE FIRST ATOMIC BOMB DROPPED?

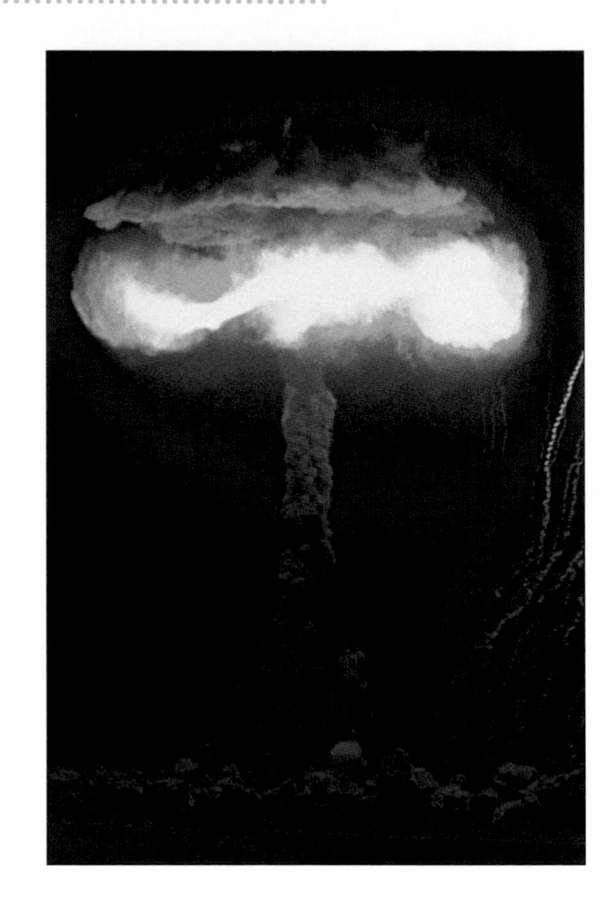

Technological advances in the weapons of war were rapid during the 20th century. During World War I, inventions included the tank and the fighter aircraft. At sea, one of the major advances in military marine technology happened before the war, with the building of the battleship *Dreadnought*.

During World War II, the Germans used a new type of warfare, known as *blitzkreig* (lightning war). In the United States, the atomic bomb was invented.

The first atomic bomb exploded in an experiment in New Mexico in July 1945. A month later, atomic bombs were used to end World War II. Atomic bombs were dropped on Japan, killing about 130,000 people. Many people suffered effects, such as radiation and burn injuries. This bomb was used to bring the war against Japan to a catastrophic end.

FACT FILE

Both the British and the French armies experimented with tanks during World War I. These armored vehicles were first used in the Battle of Cambrai in 1917.

WHEN DID INDIA GAIN INDEPENDENCE?

FACT FILE

Mohandas Gandhi was known as Mahatma Gandhi. He was assassinated in 1948, at the end of India's long struggle for independence.

Many Indians wanted independence from British rule. They also wanted a chance to build up industry and wealth in India. By the end of World War II, it was clear that Britain could no longer ignore the demands of the people in India. But negotiations were complicated by the demands of the Muslims in India. Violence broke out between Hindus and Muslims, and Indian and British leaders eventually agreed to divide India into the two states of Hindu India and Muslim Pakistan.

India gained its independence in August of 1947. Millions of Hindus and Muslims fled from their homes. As people tried to move to new homes, hundreds of thousands of people were killed.

WHEN WAS COFFEE FIRST BREWED?

The first coffee plants were probably cultivated in Kaffa, a province of Ethiopia in East Africa. Here, the beans had been used as an edible stimulant for centuries, roasted or prepared with fat.

Coffee first appeared to be brewed as a drink in the Yemen in the fourteenth century. As Muslims, they found the stimulating effects of coffee an alternative to wine. From the Yemen, the use of coffee spread to the rest of the Islamic world. It first appeared in Western Europe around 1615.

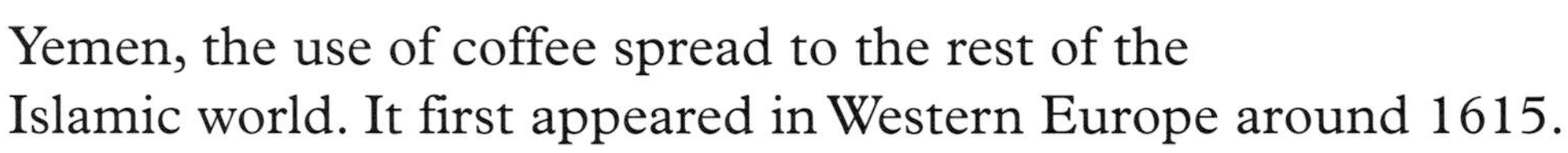

Coffee is now grown widely in tropical regions, especially in Colombia, the Ivory Coast, and Brazil, which is the world's largest producer. The coffee plants are pruned to about ten feet. This makes it easier to harvest the berries, each of which holds two tough-skinned greenish beans. After six or seven months, the beans ripen to a deep red and are ready for picking. The richness and strength of the resulting coffee depends on the variety of beans and the length of time for which they are roasted.

FACT FILE

Tea is another popular beverage. The Chinese are the original tea drinkers. They have enjoyed tea for more than 4,000 years. It was only about 300 years ago that Europeans first tasted tea.

WHEN WERE THE FIRST COINS MADE?

FACT FILE

New England shillings were the first currency in America. The English government strictly regulated the coinage.

The first coins were made in the seventh century by the Lydians in Asia Minor. They had fixed proportions of silver and gold. The coins were stamped with the issuing authority's symbol to avoid forgery. They were about the size and shape of a bean and were known as "staters" or "standards."

The Greeks and Romans adopted the idea. Roman coins were usually stamped with the head of the current emperor on one side and a mythological subject on the other. They were also dated. So, Roman archaeologists find coins very useful in helping them date other finds.

A selection of coins

When was the crossword puzzle invented?

The first crossword puzzle, in the modern sense, appeared in a Sunday copy of the New York *World* on December 21, 1913.

The modern crossword is made of a number of interlocking words within a frame of black and white squares. Each word corresponds to a numbered clue.

1 P	A	2 R	R	3 O	4 T	
A		E		5 R	O	6 E
7 C	A	S	E	D		N
K		T		I		D
E		8 O	U	N	C	E
9 T	A	R		A		A
	10 S	E	L	L	E	R

Before this, puzzles had included square puzzles in which letters spelled the same word horizontally and acrostics in which a series of answers laid out one above the other would reveal another related word running vertically.

There are now many variations on crossword puzzles.

FACT FILE

Another type of popular puzzle is the jigsaw puzzle. This is a picture which is printed onto cardboard and then cut into many pieces. These pieces interlock so that you can recreate the picture.

WHEN WERE THE FIRST SKYSCRAPERS BUILT?

Today, in industrial cities all over the world, you will see very tall buildings. The first of these buildings were erected in the nineteenth century. Because of the crowded nature of cities, buildings needed to be as tall as possible in order to maximize space. They could be made taller because of the improvements in construction using steel frames, which made tall buildings both stronger and lighter than stone buildings. In 1883, the Home Insurance Building became the first skyscraper in the United States.

FACT FILE

For hundreds of years, cathedrals were the tallest structures in the world. Tall spires were added to bring the building "closer to God."

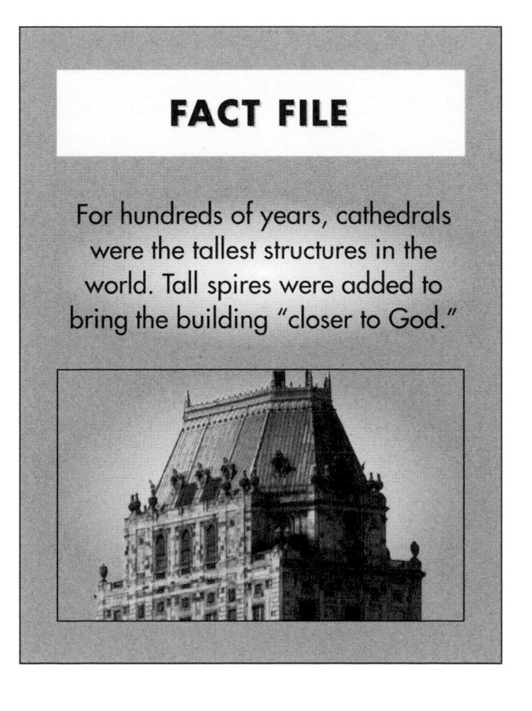

WHEN WERE THE SIGNS OF THE ZODIAC RECOGNIZED?

Capricorn

Recognition of the constellations in the sky can be traced back to early civilizations. The Chinese and Babylonians both had their own systems for making patterns in the stars. The area of the zodiac was special because the sun, moon, and planets always traveled in this part of the sky. Over the course of 12 months, the sun would travel around this band. So, the band was divided into 12 sections, each with its own constellation. We know these constellations as Aries, Taurus, Gemini, Cancer, Leo, Virgo, Libra, Scorpio, Sagittarius, Capricorn, Aquarius, and Pisces.

Scorpio

Pisces

The oldest record of the zodiacal signs appears in a horoscope from 419 B.C. As well as for astrological purposes, ancient people used the apparent movement of the sun and moon relative to the background of the zodiac to help plan the annual cycle of sowing and harvesting crops.

FACT FILE

In addition to the 12 constellations of the zodiac, 36 other constellations were recognized by people of ancient times. These 48 are known as the ancient constellations.

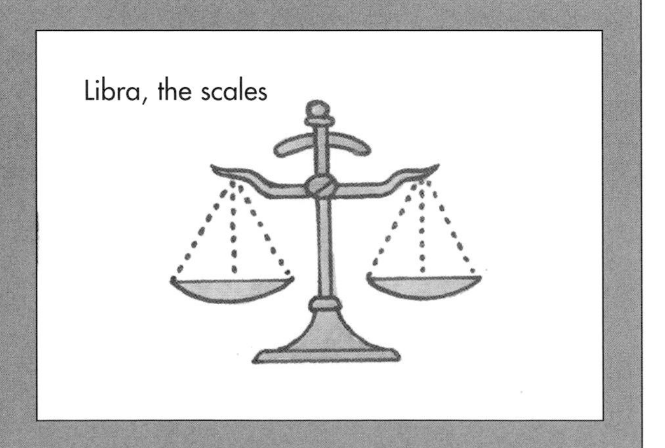

Libra, the scales

WHEN WAS THE SYDNEY OPERA HOUSE BUILT?

The Sydney Opera House in Australia is the busiest performing arts center in the world. Construction of this building started in March 1959 and proceeded in slow stages over the next fourteen years. Since its opening in 1973, it has brought countless hours of entertainment to millions of people and has continued to attract the best in world class talent year after year. In an average year, the Sydney Opera House presents plays, musicals, opera, contemporary dance, ballet, every form of music from symphony concerts to jazz, as well as exhibitions and films.

FACT FILE

The original design of the opera house called for two auditoriums. The government changed its mind, and it was built with four. Recently, it is being updated to have five.

WHEN DID BALLET BEGIN?

Ballet has been the dominant style in Western dance since its development in the 17th century. Its characteristic style of movement is still based on the positions and steps developed in the court dances of the 16th and 17th centuries.

The most basic feature of the ballet style is the turned-out position of the legs and feet. The head is nearly always lifted, and the arms are held out in extended curves. The body is always held erect, apart from controled arches in the back or a slight turning of the shoulders.

Ballet has undergone many stylistic alterations. The Romantic style of the early to mid-19th century was much softer. It did not involve as many jumps and turns as the classical style of the late 19th and early 20th centuries. Russian ballet is often regarded as the model of the classical school. It is a mixture of various styles, including the athleticism of Russian folk dances.

FACT FILE

Ballet dancers wear special shoes. These shoes have wooden blocks around the toes to enable a dancer to perform many complicated moves on the tips of the toes.

WHEN WERE BUTTONS FIRST USED?

The use of buttons appears to go back to the beginning of history. Objects, like animal teeth, would have been stitched to cloth and then pushed through a corresponding hole to form a simple, yet effective fastening. However, there are some parts of the world that have never used buttons.

In the middle ages, buttons began to be used to hold clothing together, instead the use of brooches. Buttons have never gone out of fashion since. The invention of the zipper in the first part of the 20th century lessened the button's popularity. Most buttons are now made of plastic.

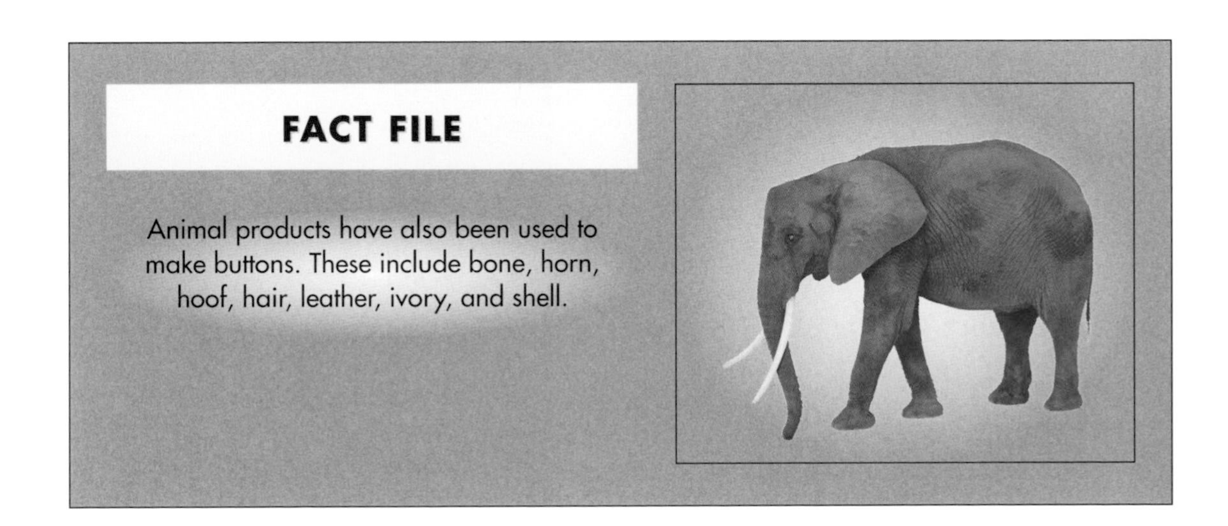

FACT FILE

Animal products have also been used to make buttons. These include bone, horn, hoof, hair, leather, ivory, and shell.

WHEN WERE CATS DOMESTICATED?

Cats were domesticated probably about 5,000 years ago, but it is hard to tell where this first happened. Today's domesticated cats, in all different breeds and color variations, are probably the descendants of two or three types of small wildcats that existed in Europe, North Africa, and Asia.

The Egyptians had tame cats 4,000 years ago. In Europe, however, there were probably no tame cats until after 1000 A.D. because they were regarded with suspicion and thought to be associated with witches.

FACT FILE

Egyptians worshipped the cat as a god. Their goddess Bast, or Pacht, was shown in pictures with a cat's head. Sacrifices were offered to cats and sacred cats were mummified.

When did the tradition of Easter eggs begin?

Many Easter traditions stem back to pre-Christian traditions. For ancient people, the coming of spring represented new life. The ancient Egyptians and Persians celebrated spring festivals by painting and eating eggs, as they still do in parts of Europe today. This is because they considered the egg as a symbol of fertility and new life. The early Christians also adopted the egg as a symbol of new life or of the Resurrection.

Until recently, eggs were forbidden food during Lent, the 40 day period before Easter. This was because they came from chickens. When Lent ended, people were glad to see and eat eggs again. They made it a tradition to eat them on Easter Sunday.

Chocolate Easter eggs are a 20th century adaption of this age-old custom.

FACT FILE

In ancient Egyptian and Celtic legends, the rabbit was associated with the moon. It became a symbol of a new period of life. The Christians, therefore, linked the rabbit with Easter.

WHEN WAS THE FIRST LIGHTHOUSE BUILT?

Before lighthouses, there were beacon fires kindled on hilltops. The earliest references to these are in the epic poems the *Iliad* and the *Odyssey* by Homer. The first authenticated man-made lighthouse was the *Pharos of Alexandria*, which stood 350 feet (about 100 m) tall. The Romans erected many lighthouse towers in the course of expanding their empire. By 400 A.D., there were 30 in service from the Black Sea to the Atlantic. These included lighthouses at Boulogne, France, and Dover, England. A fragment of the original Roman lighthouse at Dover still exists.

FACT FILE

Early lighthouses burned wood fires, sometimes protected by a roof. After the first century A.D., candles or oil lamps were used in lanterns with panes of glass.

When did oranges first arrive in America?

The Spanish brought oranges, lemon, and grapefruit to Florida and the West Indies, but they were used as ornamental trees not as food. By the end of the 19th century, all three fruits were being shipped north to New England from Florida and California.

Oranges are believed to be native to the tropical regions of Asia, especially the Malay Archipelago. Oranges, along with other citrus fruits, have been cultivated from remote ages. Orange culture probably spread from its native habitat to India and the east coast of Africa and from there to the eastern Mediterranean region. The Roman conquests, the development of Arab trade routes, and the expansion of Islam contributed greatly to their dispersal. By the time Christopher Columbus set sail, orange trees were common in the Canary Islands, and lemon trees were common in the former Arabic lands of southern Spain. Today, oranges are cultivated in subtropical and tropical areas in America, northern and eastern Mediterranean countries, Australia, and South Africa. Oranges thrive best where the trees are chilled by occasional light frosts in winter.

FACT FILE

Orange orchards are generally planted in deep soil where drainage is good. They thrive in a wide range of soil conditions.

When was wallpaper first used?

Wallpaper developed soon after the introduction of papermaking to Europe. This was during the later part of the 15th century. Although it is often assumed that the Chinese invented wallpaper, there is no evidence that it was in general use in Asia any earlier than the time of its appearance in Europe. The earliest wallpapers in England and France were hand painted or stenciled. During the 17th century, decorative techniques also included block printing and flocking. Flocking is a process where powdered wool or metallic powders are scattered over paper on which a design has been drawn with a slow-drying adhesive. The oldest existing example of flocked wallpaper comes from Worcester and was created in approximately 1680.

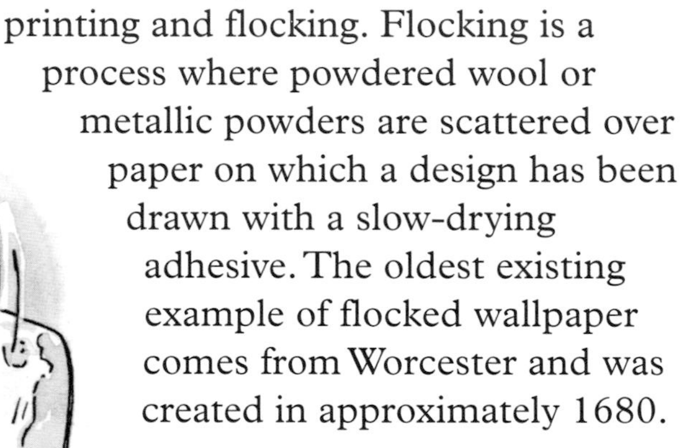

FACT FILE

Wallpaper designs of the artist William Morris (1834-1896) exist today. His style is very distinct, and his work is much sought-after.

When was the internal combustion engine developed?

Though best known for his invention of the diesel engine, French-born Rudolf Diesel was also an eminent thermal engineer, a connoisseur of the arts, a linguist, and a social theorist. During 1885, Diesel set up his first laboratory in Paris and began his 13-year ordeal of creating his distinctive engine. At Augsburg, on August 10, 1893, Diesel's first model, a single ten-foot iron cylinder with a flywheel at its base, ran on its own power for the first time. Diesel spent two more years working on improvements, and on the last day of 1896, he demonstrated another model with the spectacular mechanical efficiency of 75.6 percent. His engines were used to power pipelines, electric and water plants, automobiles, trucks, and marine craft. They were also later used in applications including mines, oil fields, factories, and transoceanic shipping.

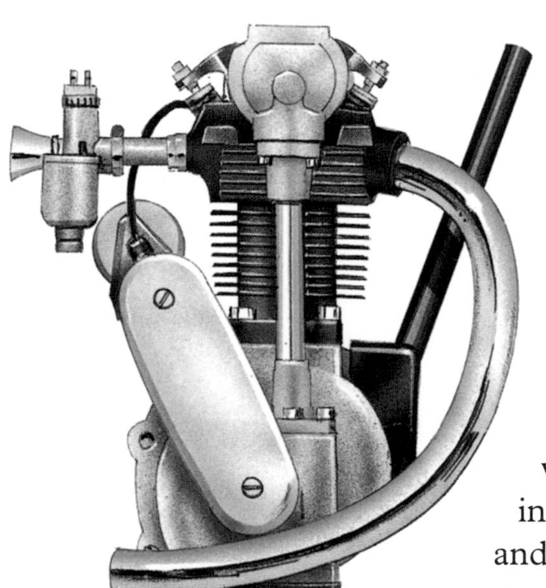

FACT FILE

Originally, Diesel conceived the combustion engine as an alternative to the oversized, expensive, fuel-wasting steam engine, which was being widely used in industry.

When were wedding rings first worn?

The tradition of a bride wearing a wedding ring dates back so far that its origins are obscure.

We know that the Egyptians wore wedding rings. In hieroglyphics, a circle is the symbol of eternity. So, a wedding ring indicated an unending and indivisible bond. The wedding ring made its first appearance in Christianity in about 900 A.D.

Some people see a more negative history to the wedding ring and believe that it is a diminutive version of the slave band bracelet or neck collar that captive women wore in prehistoric times to indicate that they were someone else's property. Now, the wearing of wedding rings is practized in almost all cultures, often by men as well as women.

Gold is the traditional metal for wedding rings, because it does not tarnish. So, it is also a symbol of everlasting marriage.

FACT FILE

In most cultures, the ring is worn on the fourth finger of the left hand. Supposedly, this is because the ancient Greeks believed a vein passed from this finger directly to the heart. However, it is more likely that it is simply because the fourth finger of the left hand is not used very much.

WHEN DID WEDDINGS BEGIN?

Marriage has a long history in all cultures of the world. A long time ago, a man would simply steal the woman he wanted from her family. Roman legend says that the early Romans acquired their wives by taking them from their neighbors, the Sabines.

Then, marriage by contract or purchase was practized. A bride was bought from her family by a man. This was succeeded by arranged marriages. In the upper social classes, wealth and social status were important. Lower down on the social scale, it was not uncommon for apprentices to marry into their master's families and end up inheriting part of the business.

FACT FILE

The custom of tying shoes to the back of newlyweds' cars is believed to go back to the exchanging of shoes that indicated authority had been exchanged. So, the shoe suggests that the husband has authority over the bride.

Finally, in Western culture, marriage based on mutual love was practized. Echoes of earlier traditions still exist however, even though the best man no longer has to help his friend break into a home and steal the bride. Brides are now "given away" rather than sold. It is now also becoming increasingly common for the bridal couple to contribute to the costs of their own wedding, rather than expecting the bride's father to pay the whole cost of the ceremony and celebration.

WHEN WAS HONEY FIRST USED?

Honey has been used as a sweetener since very ancient times. It was practically the only way early man could get sugar. Honey is mentioned in the Bible, the Koran, and by Homer, as well as many other Greek writers.

In Egypt, it is recorded as being used as a medicine, embalming fluid, and as a paste for cosmetics, such as the black kohl they used around their eyes. It was used throughout history to make a sweet strong beer called *mead* and to sweeten wine. In ancient India, it was used to preserve and sweeten foods.

Scientists have not yet managed to recreate honey in a laboratory. There have been concerns about future supplies of honey because of a parasitic mite called *Varroa*. Varroa preys upon bees until the hive dies. The northward sweep of killer bees in southern North America and the aggressive, less productive African bees in Europe are also concerns.

FACT FILE

Honeybees tell other worker bees in the colony where good sources of food can be found. They do this by performing a special dance, called *the honey dance*, on their return to the hive.

WHEN DID BOXING BEGIN?

FACT FILE

Baseball is another popular sport. In 1839, the first baseball diamond was supposedly laid out by an American named Abner Doubleday in Cooperstown, New York.

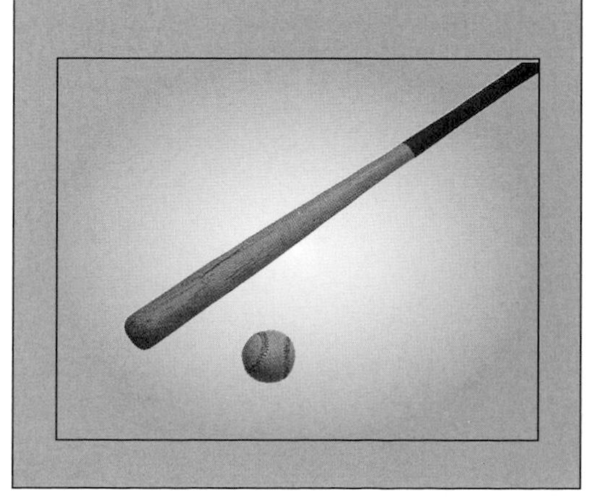

Boxing appeared in England at the beginning of the eighteenth century. Going to watch and bet on prize fights became a fashionable pursuit, and it has remained so for more than 200 years. Gentlemen in the eighteenth century kept themselves fit by sparring in boxing saloons. But the sport has a far longer tradition than that. Boxers, who wore heavy gloves on their hands, are known to have performed at Olympic games and other public events in ancient Greece and in the Roman Empire.

WHEN WERE THE FIRST HOUSES BUILT?

FACT FILE

Ice Age hunters made shelters from the bones of mammoths. They made the framework out of bones and filled in the gaps with skins, turf, and moss.

Many early people took refuge in caves, but as people spread out through regions where there were no caves, they had to find alternatives. Hunters made tents from animal skins. Other people made huts from interwoven twigs and plastered mud in the gaps to keep the wind out. Straw was used on the roof to stop the rain.

The ancient Egyptians are believed to have been among the first to make sun-dried mud bricks. In Mesopotamia, people developed a way of making bricks stronger and more durable by placing them in a hot fire and firing them. In places like Babylon, bricks have lasted for thousands of years.

WHEN WAS THE SHANG DYNASTY?

The Shang dynasty was the earliest known Chinese family of rulers. The dynasty governed from the sixteenth to eleventh centuries B.C.

Its central point was in the area now known as the northern Henan Province in the valley of the Huang He (the Yellow River). Shang society was based on agriculture. Because of their perfection of irrigation techniques, the kings became wealthy and a beautiful tradition of bronze work grew up as well. They used bronze for decorative objects, chariot fixtures, and a wide variety of weapons. Most Shang relics came from Anyang, a Shang capital, which had royal palaces, houses, temples, and elaborate tombs. Beautiful marble and jade carvings have also been found by archaeologists dating back to this time period.

Shang food vessel

FACT FILE

The Shang scribes perfected the early form of the Chinese alphabet. Their version had more than 3,000 symbols.

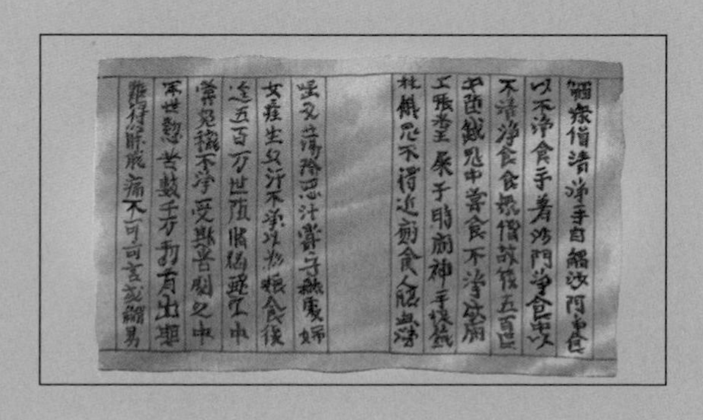

WHERE?

CONTENTS

WHERE DOES THE WORD *HISTORY* COME FROM?

History comes from a Greek word meaning *what is known by asking*. The job of a historian is to ask questions and make sense of the answers.

The Greeks were among the first people to write history based on first-hand reporting of the facts. Herodotus (who died in 425 B.C.) wrote about the wars between the Greeks and the Persians. He traveled and talked to people who had taken part in the wars.

Historians work from a viewpoint. The first people to write their own history were the Chinese. We know the name of one early Chinese historian, Sima Qian, who wrote a history of China in about 100 B.C. Early historians felt it was important to write down the stories and legends of the past and to show how their state had come into existence. Sometimes, people who made history also wrote about it. Julius Caesar, the Roman general, wrote his own book about his campaigns in Gaul.

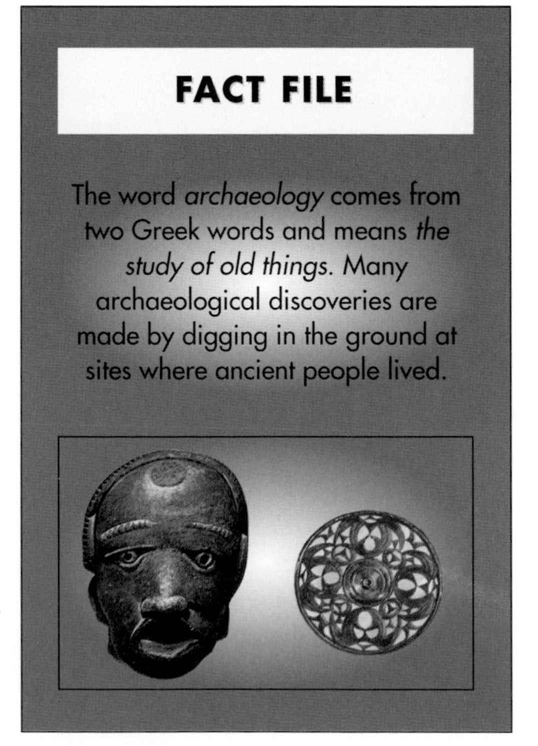

FACT FILE

The word *archaeology* comes from two Greek words and means *the study of old things*. Many archaeological discoveries are made by digging in the ground at sites where ancient people lived.

Where would you see a home of mammoth bones?

Around 18,000 years ago, the last of a series of Ice Ages gripped much of the Northern Hemisphere. Icecaps spread southward across Europe and North America. The sea level fell, uncovering land bridges, which animals and people crossed. One such land bridge was between Asia and Alaska.

Ice Age hunters, clothed only in animal skins, adapted to living in these freezing conditions. They built shelters from the bones of mammoths. They made the framework of the shelters from bones and filled in the gaps with skins, turf, and moss. Groups of men drove the animals into swamps, where they became trapped and were killed with spears or rocks.

FACT FILE

Tools for scraping the skins of animals were made mostly from flint. This hard material could be chipped into tools of many different shapes and sizes.

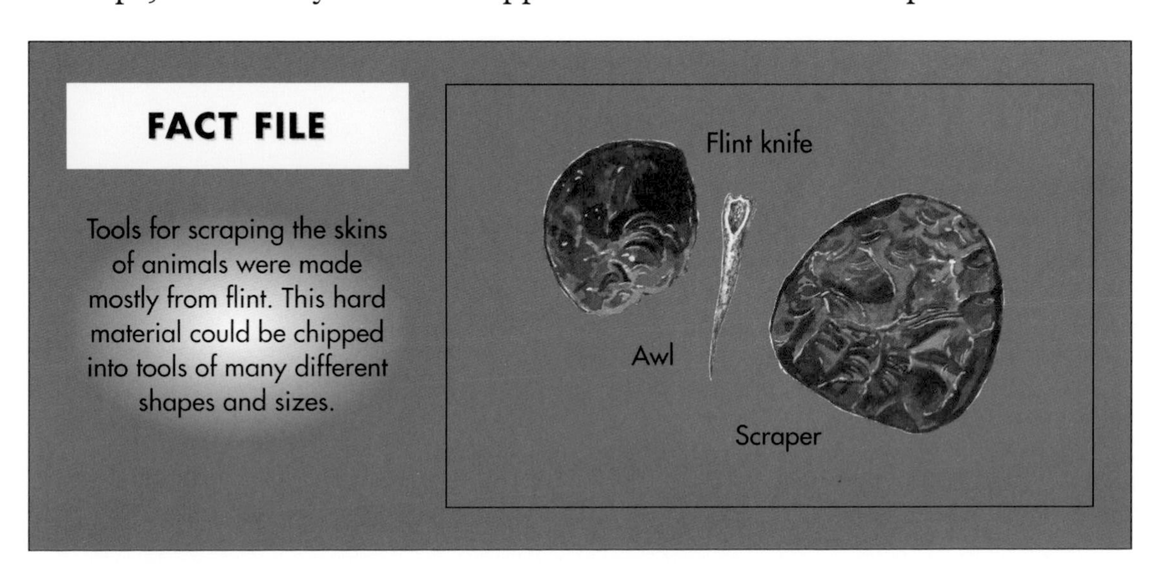

WHERE WAS SUMER?

Mesopotamia, meaning *between rivers*, lay in the country we now know as modern Iraq. Northern Mesopotamia's weather was mild, with enough rain to grow crops in some areas. In the south, lay a flat, swampy plain built up from the mud spread by the river floodwaters. This area was called *Sumer.* It received little rain and had long, hot summers. People had lived in Sumer since 5000 B.C. They fished the rivers, hunted wild pigs and birds for food, and picked fruit from date palms. The muddy soil was rich, but crops died without rain in the burning summer heat. So, farmers dug canals to channel river water to their fields of barley, wheat, dates, and vegetables. They turned over the earth with ploughs pulled by oxen.

Skilled metalworkers in Sumer made fine trinkets from silver and gold. These items were inlaid with precious stones, such as lapis lazuli.

Sumerian robes

Sumer body adornments

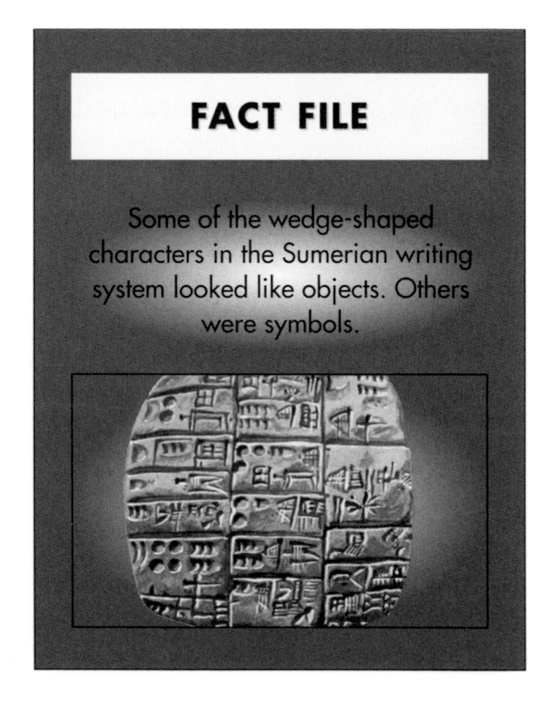

FACT FILE

Some of the wedge-shaped characters in the Sumerian writing system looked like objects. Others were symbols.

WHERE DID SARGON OF AKKAD BUILD HIS EMPIRE?

Sargon of Akkad's empire was centered on Mesopotamia in the twenty-fourth century B.C. Many historians classify it as the first truly important empire in history. Although not apparently of royal blood, Sargon was cupbearer to the king of Kish, a great general and administrator. By the end of his 56 years in power, the bureaucracy of his empire was so well organized that it did not fall until 60 years after his death.

Sargon conquered Kish and the other Sumerian city states one by one. He was one of the first people with imperial ambitions who understood that you needed to be able to trust the men you left in charge of conquered cities. So, he appointed people from his own court rather than locals who would rebel as soon as he turned his back.

Sargon expanded his empire to what is now Iran in the east and to the Mediterranean and Asia Minor (now Turkey) in the west.

FACT FILE

Sargon made one of his daughters a priestess of the moon god in Ur. The royal standard of Ur, a decorated wooden box, dates from about 2500 B.C. On its mosaic panels, farmers parade and soldiers march into battle.

WHERE WAS THE WORLD'S FIRST GREAT CIVILIZATION?

The Indus Valley civilization developed out of farming and herding communities in the rich, fertile lands of the river valley. These lands carried on trade with each other. The civilization appears to have been based on cooperation rather than military might.

It began to flourish around 4,500 years ago in the vast river plains of what are now Pakistan and northwestern India. Cities began to develop about 2,000 years later, with Harappa in the north and Mohenjo Daro in the south. There was certainly a degree of central control because they were both carefully planned cities, laid out on a grid system. The wealth of the valley people is obvious from the amenities in the cities, which had communal water supplies, wide roads, and brick houses with more than one floor. Most homes had a bathing area, which was unheard of anywhere else at that time.

FACT FILE

The farmers of the Indus Valley used wooden carts pulled by oxen. Deep grooves made by heavy carts have been found in the excavated streets of Mohenjo Daro.

WHERE DID KING ASHURBANIPAL RULE?

Assyria, an ancient state on the upper Tigris River in Mesopotamia, was ruled from 668 to 627 B.C. by a king called Ashurbanipal. Assyria lay to the north of Babylon, a city with which it had many cultural similarities. It is occupied roughly the area of the northern half of Iraq. Ashurbanipal's capital was in Nineveh, where he had a magnificent palace, a library, and ornate gardens. Although damaged and vandalized, some of the ruins are still visible today.

King Ashurbanipal

Ashurbanipal was, like all Assyrian kings, an absolute ruler. He was the representative on earth of their chief god, Assur.

The Assyrian empire was at its height during the early part of Ashurbanipal's reign. But in 1651 B.C., the Egyptians started to rebel against his rule. Then, just three years later, the Babylonians did the same thing, weakening his powers even further. After his death in 627 B.C., Babylonia invaded and then overtook Egypt as well. This period is thought to have been when the Hebrews were exiled to Babylon.

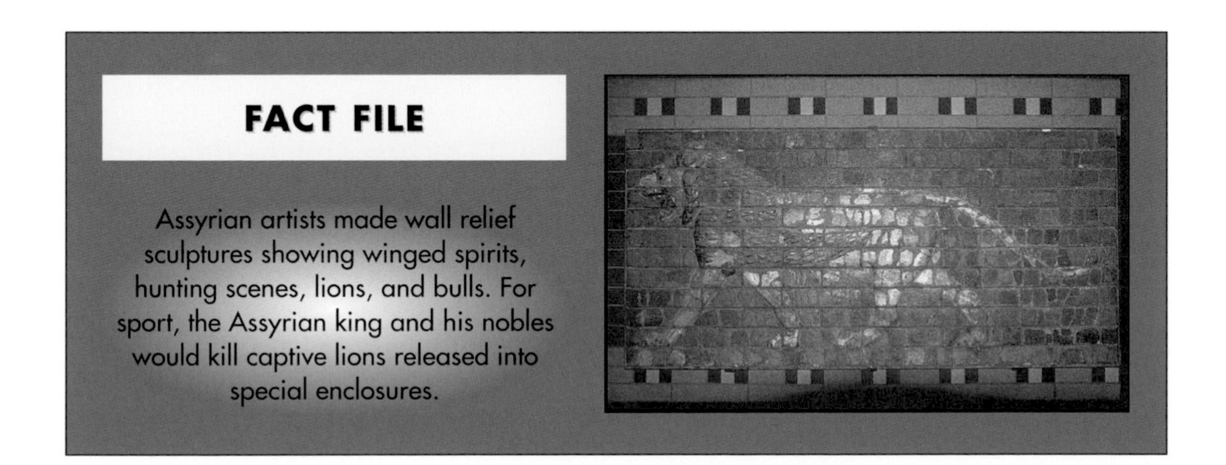

FACT FILE

Assyrian artists made wall relief sculptures showing winged spirits, hunting scenes, lions, and bulls. For sport, the Assyrian king and his nobles would kill captive lions released into special enclosures.

WHERE ARE THE RUINS OF PERSEPOLIS?

FACT FILE

Ten thousand soldiers, called the *Immortals*, formed the core of the Persian army. Each spearman or archer was instantly replaced if killed.

Persepolis laid in the southwest area of what is now Iran, in a strategic position in the mountains. It was built as one of his capitals by King Darius I of Persia around 500 B.C. Large stone and mud brick palaces were built, and the city became the royal ceremonial area for the new year's religious rituals. This was when Darius and his successors would renew their divine rights as kings and expect gifts from all the client kings of the empire.

In 330 B.C., having already defeated the last Persian king, Alexander the Great seized Persepolis, and the city's life came to an end. Archaeologists have uncovered many of the ruins. Some of these ruins have been restored, and visitors are able to see some of the buildings of the King's great palace.

WHERE WAS THE BATTLE OF SALAMIS?

Salamis is a Greek island in the Saronic Gulf, about ten miles west of Athens. It is rocky, bare, and mountainous.

During the early fifth century B.C., the Athenians were trying to throw off the rule of the Persian empire. Ten years earlier, they had defeated them on land at the Battle of Marathon. Now, it was the turn of the Athenian fleet to inflict damage on Darius I. In 480 B.C., the Greeks ambushed the Persian ships in the strait between Salamis and the mainland. They fought a great sea battle near Salamis. Arrows, stones, and spears rained between the ships, but the Greek's key weapon was the ramming power of their galleys. The Persian ships tried to block the retreat of Greek vessels, but the Greeks still managed to destroy half of the Persian fleet.

FACT FILE

Broken pieces of pottery were used for letter-writing in the Greek world.

WHERE DID THE GREAT RELIGIONS OF THE WORLD BEGIN?

Four-armed Vishnu

All the great religions of the world began in Asia. Three of them–Judaism, Christianity and Islam–began in the same area of west Asia. Hinduism and Buddhism began in India. People all over the world formed a system of belief in powers greater than their own. The earliest religions were connected with the forces of nature–the sun, the moon, wind, water, rocks, and trees–and with animals. Hinduism is the oldest of the Asian beliefs. There are many Hindu gods and rules governing food, conduct, festivals, and even the jobs people do. Hindu sculptures of gods and goddesses are full of energy. The four-armed Vishnu is the preserver of the universe. He is one of Hinduism's two main gods. The other god is Shiva.

Buddhism began in India in the 500s B.C. and was later spread by missionaries to Burma and China. In its birthplace of India, Buddhism has practicaly died out.

FACT FILE

Hindu pilgrims went to bathe in the waters of the holy river Ganges. This tradition is still carried on to this day.

A bronze statue of Buddha

WHERE DOES THE NAME *DRUID* COME FROM?

The name *druid* is derived from *oak*. *Dru-wid* combines the root words *oak* and *knowledge*. Pliny the Elder in his work *Naturalis Historia* (XVI 95), associated the druids with mistletoe and oak groves:

> "The druids . . . hold nothing more sacred than the mistletoe and the tree on which it grows provided it is an oak. They choose the oak to form groves, and they do not perform any religious rites without its foliage . . ."

Celtic priests, also known as druids, have often been identified as wizards and soothsayers. They performed mysterious rites in sacred groves of trees. The moon, the oak, and the mistletoe were all magical to the druids, as were many animals. However, in pre-Christian Celtic society, druids formed an intellectual class comprising of philosophers, judges, educators, historians, doctors, seers, astronomers and astrologers. The earliest surviving classical references to druids date to the second century B.C.

FACT FILE

Around a campfire at night, Celtic poets, storytellers, and musicians would pass on tales of the gods and events in the history of the Celtic people.

WHERE WAS ETRURIA?

Etruria was an area of Italy, known today as Tuscany, Umbria, and Latium. Etruria originally extended from the Arno in the north to the Tiber in the south and from the Apennines in the east to the Tyrrhenian Sea in the west. The people of Etruria were a highly organized, militaristic society, who rapidly extended their territories north across the Apennines into the Po Valley and south across the Tiber River into Latium and Campania. The civilization reached its height in the 400s B.C. The Etruscans lost control of Rome in 510 B.C. when the last Etruscan king, Tarquinius Superbus, was driven out, leaving Rome a republic. Rome is thought to have obtained many of its military techniques from the Etruscans.

FACT FILE

Part of a carved stone relief depicting a Roman funeral procession is shown below. The pallbearers carried the dead person on a raised bier, followed by the mourners.

WHERE WERE THE FIRST GLADIATOR GAMES HELD?

Records state that the first gladiator games were held to commemorate the funeral of a Roman aristocrat in a cattle market in 264 B.C. There were many venues for fights, but the most famous one, the Colosseum in Rome, was built between 72 to 81 A.D. by the emperor Vespasian. There, wild beasts fought in the morning, and the gladiators fought in the afternoon.

Gladiators were highly trained and fought using many different types of weapons, for example a shield and sword or a net and long trident. They usually fought until one gladiator was killed, but the life of the loser could be spared if the spectators waved handkerchiefs or if the emperor gave him the thumbs-up, rather than the thumbs-down.

FACT FILE

Most gladiators were prisoners of war, slaves, or criminals. Slaves wore tags advertising their skills and good character to enhance their price at auction.

WHERE DID THE ROMANS BATHE?

Only wealthy Romans could afford to own private baths, but the city had many public ones. During the time of the emperors, the public baths became luxurious meeting places. They looked like great square-shaped swimming pools and were surrounded by gardens, columned marbles porches, and libraries. The bath buildings had facilities for warm and cold baths, steam baths, and massages.

The most splendid remains of baths in Rome are those of Caracalla and Diocletian. The Baths of Caracalla date from the early 200s A.D. and are especially impressive. They were decorated with precious marble, statues, and mosaics. The Baths of Diocletian, completed in the early 300s A.D., were the largest of all Roman baths. They could serve 3,000 people at one time. Most of the site has been built over, but some rooms can still be seen.

FACT FILE

A Roman villa was a large comfortable country home, with hot-air central heating and a courtyard for nice weather. The family had servants to run the house and slaves to work on the land.

WHERE DID CHARIOT RACES TAKE PLACE?

A Hippodrome was the place where horse and chariot races occurred. The Greeks built hippodromes with seats in rows, or tiers, surrounding a long race course, curving around one end of it. The course was usually from 590 to 787 feet long and could be divided in the middle by a wall. The largest Greek hippodrome was in Constantinople (now Istanbul). The Roman Circus Maximus, the largest of all Roman hippodromes, was a copy of the Greek originals. It seated around 250,000 spectators. The layout of one of Domitian's hippodromes can still be seen in the street plan of the Piazza Navona in Rome. The chariot races were known for their frequent violent crashes, and winning drivers became rich superstars. The emperor Caligula is said to have enjoyed racing, especially since he always won.

FACT FILE

In a Greek theater, the actors performed on a flat platform called the *orchestra*. Audiences sat in the open air on a hillside. Audiences might watch as many as four plays in a single day.

WHERE WAS THE SILK ROAD?

The Silk Road was a group of ancient trade routes that connected China and Europe. It was a concept rather than a physical road and flourished primarily from 100 B.C. to 1500 A.D. The routes stretched across about 5,002 miles from the Mediterranean, across Arabia, through India and what is now Burma to the far edge of China.

The Silk Road was named after the vast amounts of Chinese silk that were carried along it, but parts of it had been trade routes for thousands of years before. Towns and cities sprang up along the route to provide facilities for food, water, and recreation, as well as goods for trade. This trade made a number of countries very rich, as the merchants had to pass through to avoid being attacked by bandits. Other goods sold included gold, spices, and jewelery. Camel caravans carried most goods across the dry, harsh regions along the Silk Road.

By 800 A.D., with the Ottoman empire in turmoil, traffic fell as traders started to travel by safer sea routes.

FACT FILE

The Chinese were the first to learn to make silk, and they guarded their secret. They had a monopoly on silk until the 500s A.D., when a merchant is thought to have smuggled some silk worms back in a hollow cane.

WHERE WAS THE BIGGEST GROWTH OF THE MUSLIM EMPIRE?

The advance of Islam seemed unstoppable in the late 600s. The Byzantine and Persian empires could not halt the armies of Islam, nor could Egypt. By 700 A.D., Muslims controled most of the North African coast and ships patroled the Mediterranean Sea and Indian Ocean. Muslims from Morocco invaded Spain, but the advance of Islam into western Europe was stopped in 732 A.D. by the Frankish army of Charles Martel. Under the Muslim Ummayad family rule, there were four classes of citizens: Arabian Muslims; new converts; Christians, Jews, and Mandaens (a Persian sect); and slaves. The new converts included people from Egypt, Syria, Persia, and Asia Minor. They adopted Arab ways but brought to the Arabs a wealth of new learning in philosophy, medicine, art, and science.

FACT FILE

The crescent moon and star became important symbols in Islam and were often incorporated into architecture and other designs.

A scene from "The Thousand and One Nights"

WHERE WAS THE BATTLE OF CRÉCY?

The Battle of Crécy was the first important battle of the Hundred Years' War (1337 to 1453). It occured at the site of the present village of Crécy, in northern France. The Hundred Years' War began in 1337 and continued periodically for more than a century.

In this battle, English archers on foot under Edward III defeated Philip VI's much larger force of mounted knights. More than 1,000 were killed, as was almost half of the French force in the Battle of Crécy. The hero of the battle was Edward, the Black Prince, son of Edward III of England.

FACT FILE

Knights decorated their shield with the heraldic symbols of their own coat of arms. This made it easier to identify a knight in full armor. Each coat of arms had its own unique design.

WHERE ARE THE FORBIDDEN AND IMPERIAL CITIES?

The Forbidden City and the Imperial City lie within the Inner City, an area in Beijing, the capital of China. The Forbidden City includes palaces of former Chinese emperors. It was named this because only the emperor's household was allowed to enter it.

The buildings in this part of Beijing are now preserved as museums. The Imperial City surrounds the Forbidden City. It includes lakes, parks, and the residences of China's communist leaders. The Gate of Heavenly Peace stands at the southern edge of the Imperial City, overlooking Tiananmen Square.

FACT FILE

The first Ming emperor, Chu Yuan-Chang, turned Beijing into one of the greatest cities in the world, with the Forbidden City at its core.

WHERE DOES THE WORD *FEUDAL* COME FROM?

FACT FILE

Only a very wealthy person could afford costly items like this ornate gold drinking goblet. Poorer people drank out of leather tankards or earthenware cups.

Feudalism is the general term used to describe the political and military system prevalent in most of western Europe during the Middle Ages. It was a strict hierarchical system that bound everyone into one unit, with the king at the top and the peasant at the bottom. A king or lord would grant land, the fief, in return for a subject's oath of loyalty, service, and support in battle. If a knight's feudal overlord demanded help, the knight had to provide as much suport as his oath contracted him to, possibly two mounted men and four archers. The church was also part of the feudal system. Feudalism began to appear in the 700s. By the 1100s, it had spread from France into England, Spain, and other parts of the Christian world.

WHERE WAS THE FIRST PRINTING PRESS BUILT?

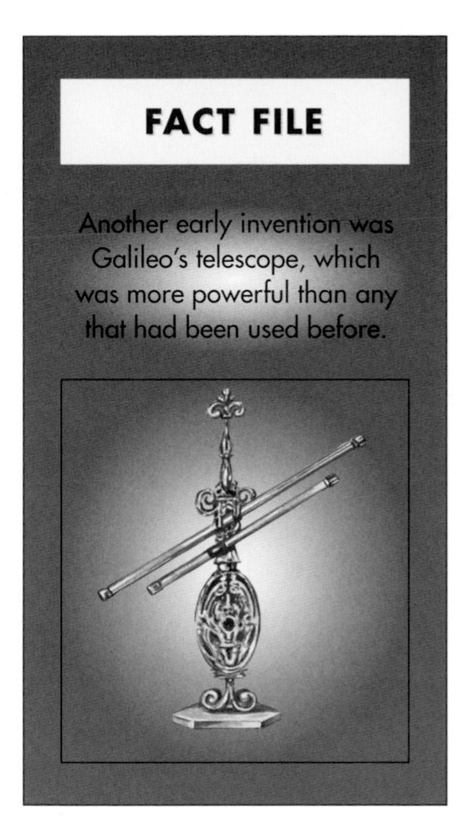

FACT FILE

Another early invention was Galileo's telescope, which was more powerful than any that had been used before.

Throughout history, books have been rare and precious objects, kept in libraries of monasteries or wealthy houses. Each book had to be copied out by hand with pen and ink. So, very few people had the chance to learn to read. The Chinese developed a simple system of printing in the eleventh century, but it was only in about 1450 that a German named Johannes Gutenberg built the first printing press. Using movable metal type, Gutenberg was able to make exact copies of books very cheaply.

The first books he printed were the Bible and other religious texts. Soon, other printers started, and by 1500, they were producing many different sorts of literature, including poems and stories. For the first time, books were available to everyone.

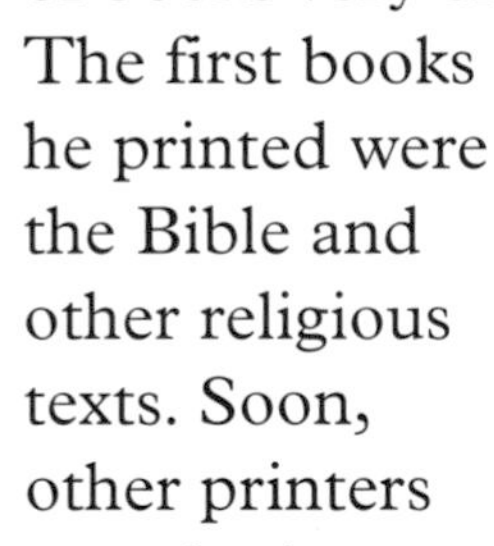

WHERE DID THE PILGRIMS FIRST LAND?

FACT FILE

In the colonies, girls would embroider samplers, squares of cloth decorated with words and patterns of needlework. They usually added their name and age, as well as the date.

Pilgrims were the early English settlers of New England. The first group of pilgrims set sail from England in 1620 on a ship called the *Mayflower*. They landed at what is now Plymouth, Massachusetts, where they established Plymouth Colony along Cape Cod Bay.

In 1606, William Brewster helped form a small Separatist congregation in Scrooby, England. Separatist groups were illegal in England, and in 1607, the Scrooby congregation tried to flee to Amsterdam, Holland, to avoid arrest. They were caught, but most of them left England the next year. In 1609, the congregation settled in the Dutch town of Leiden.

WHERE DID THE PIONEERS COME FROM?

Pioneers were thousands of ordinary people who headed west to make better lives for themselves and their children. In doing so, they pushed the frontier of the United States westward from the Appalachian Mountains to the Pacific Ocean. Pioneers wanted to improve their social and economic position. Some hoped to have more say in political affairs. Even for those who had money to buy land, good farmland was hard to find in the East. Across the Appalachians, however, settlers could obtain a plot of fertile land for a fraction of the cost. Pioneers traveled in wagons known as "prairie schooners," because their canvas tops looked rather like sails. Settlers moved along the trail in groups for both safety and companionship. There could be up to 100 wagons in a single wagon train.

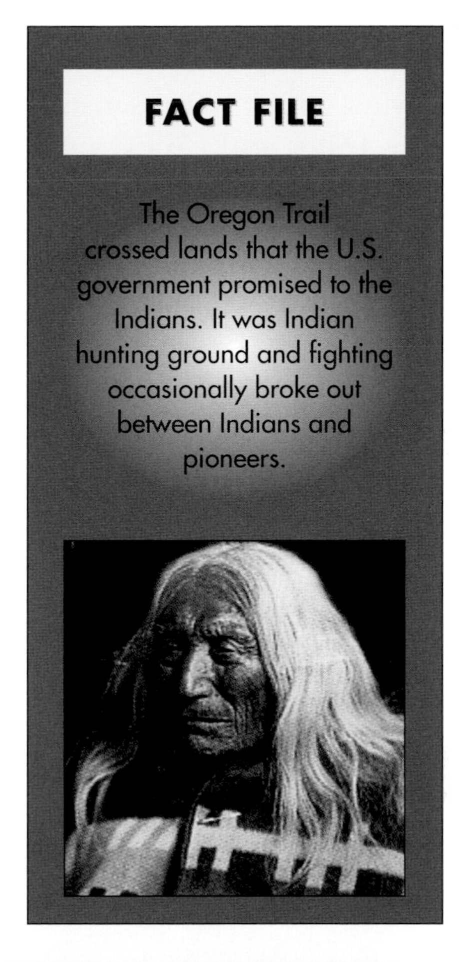

FACT FILE

The Oregon Trail crossed lands that the U.S. government promised to the Indians. It was Indian hunting ground and fighting occasionally broke out between Indians and pioneers.

WHERE WAS VOLTAIRE IMPRISONED?

Voltaire was a French philosopher and writer with a sharp sense of justice. In the 1600s and 1700s, a period called the *Age of Reason*, many people began to regard freedom of speech as a natural right. Philosophers like John Locke of England and Voltaire of France believed in the importance of the individual. Every person, they declared, had a right to speak freely and to have a voice in the government. Because of these beliefs, and for criticizing the government, Voltaire was imprisoned for eleven months in the notorious Bastille prison. The Bastille was a great fortress in Paris that stood as a symbol of royal tyranny. During his lifetime, Voltaire wrote more than 50 plays, as well as philosophical stories and poems.

FACT FILE

Voltaire was often a guest at Frederick II's court from 1750 to 1753. Frederick II was the third King of Prussia and became known as Frederick the Great.

WHERE WAS BONNIE PRINCE CHARLIE'S REBELLION?

Bonnie Prince Charlie, or Charles Edward Stuart (1720 to 1788), was the grandson of James II and the last Stuart actively to lay claim to the throne of England. Charles led his Jacobite army in a rebellion in Scotland, which turned out to be a total failure. In the late summer of 1745, Charles landed in Scotland. Many supporters joined his rebellion, especially the northern Scottish clans who resented the Hanoverian monarchy. Within weeks, he had occupied the Scottish capital, Edinburgh. By early December, Charles he had reached as far south as Derby in the English midlands. He found little support in England and cutting his losses, he retreated to Scotland. The English pursued him north, and on April 16 of the following year, his army was crushed at Culloden Moor, near Inverness. Charles hid as a fugitive in the Scottish Highlands until he managed to escape back to France in September.

FACT FILE

Bonnie Prince Charlie lead his army to victory over the English in 1745. He was born in Rome and spent the later years of his life in Italy.

WHERE WAS GENERAL JAMES WOLFE KILLED?

FACT FILE

By 1740, the number of British colonists in North America was approaching one million. Furs and other valuable goods from the colonies, such as tobacco, wood, and grain, were sold throughout Europe.

James Wolfe (1727 to 1759) was the British general whose army won the Battle of Quebec in 1759. This assured that Canada would become part of the British Empire.

Wolfe's strategy was to move his troops up the Saint Lawrence River to a landing well above the city. This brought them downriver closer to the French during the night of September 12. The battle was so decisive, it lasted only fifteen minutes. Both Wolfe and his French counterpart, General Montcalm died. Wolfe's greatness as a general has sometimes been exaggerated because he died dramatically at the moment of his greatest victory. The following year, the British army consolidated this success by taking the city of Montreal.

WHERE DID WILLIAM BUILD NORMAN CASTLES?

Conwy castle

FACT FILE

The Bayeux Tapestry was made by the Normans to celebrate their victory over the English in 1066. It is a huge series of pictures depicting incidents during the conquest.

The introduction of castles in England followed the Norman conquest of 1066. In fact, castles were the means by which William the Conqueror and his followers secured their hold on England following their victory at the battle of Hastings. William ordered castles to be built at Warwick, Nottingham, York, Lincoln, Cambridge, and Huntingdon. These defensive structures helped to secure his newly acquired lands. The first Norman castles were hurriedly constructed of earth and timber.

Conwy castle, in north Wales, is typical of the castles built by the Normans to withstand a long siege. Windsor Castle, Berkshire, is perhaps England's most famous castle.

WHERE DID THE CRUSADES TAKE PLACE?

FACT FILE

The word *crusade* comes from the Latin word *crux*, meaning *cross*. "To take up the cross" meant to become a crusader.

Crusades were military expeditions organized mainly to recapture Palestine during the Middle Ages. Palestine, also called the *Holy Land*, was important to Christians because it was the region where Jesus Christ had lived. Palestine lay along the eastern coast of the Mediterranean Sea. Muslims had taken control of it from the Christians. The crusaders, who came from Western Europe, organized eight major expeditions between 1096 and 1270 A.D. This was a period when Western Europe was expanding its economy and increasing its military forces. Kings, nobles, and thousands of knights, peasants, and townspeople took part in the crusades. They had two main goals: first, to gain permanent control of the Holy Land, and second, to protect the Byzantine empire.

WHERE WAS THE GREAT CITY OF THE ANCIENT WORLD?

One of the greatest cities of the ancient world was Babylon. It was the capital of the kingdom of Babylonia and of two Babylonian empires. Its location on the banks of the Euphrates River (near the present-day city of Al Hillah, Iraq) helped the city to become an important trading center. The first known reference of Babylon dates back to about 2200 B.C. In 1894 B.C., the first important Babylonian ruler, King Sumu-abum, founded a dynasty. King Hammurabi, who ruled from 1792 to 1750 B.C., won fame for developing a wise and fair code of law. The most famous ruler of the New Babylonian Empire was Nebuchadnezzar, who is associated with both the Babylonian exile of the Hebrews and the Hanging Gardens of Babylon.

FACT FILE

The period from 5000 to 500 B.C. was an age of crucial new technologies. The wheel, metal tools, and weapons were developed at this time. Also, coins were first used, and writing and mathematics developed. Babylonians also began to study the stars.

WHERE DID THE INDIAN TRIBES GO?

Native Americans had been living in America for thousands of years before any Europeans arrived. Indian groups had their own names, languages, belief systems, and cultures. As the Europeans moved westward across North America appropriating land, the animals the Native Americans depended on were killed. Many Native Americans were killed, and Europeans became a greater and greater threat to the Indian way of life. Most of the remaining Indians were forced onto reservations. Today, most Indians in North America still do not completely follow the ways of white people. In some areas of Central and South America, tribes have kept their language and way of life. But most Indian tribes have become part of a new way of life that is both Indian and American.

FACT FILE

Europeans passed diseases to the Indians, who had no resistance. Millions died.

Where did the Union Pacific Railroad run?

After the Civil War, the American government encouraged people to settle in the largely empty land of the Great Plains. The American Indians had already been driven out. The distances involved were enormous, and the railways were the key to opening up the huge plains of the mid-western United States, providing access for settlers and for trade. The number of locomotives and railroads multiplied rapidly in the United States after 1830. By the year 1869, the Union Pacific Railroad, which linked the east and west coasts of the United States, was finally completed. A network of other lines spread out across the plains. The railway provided an essential link between remote farming communities and cities, making it easier for people to buy goods and trade produce.

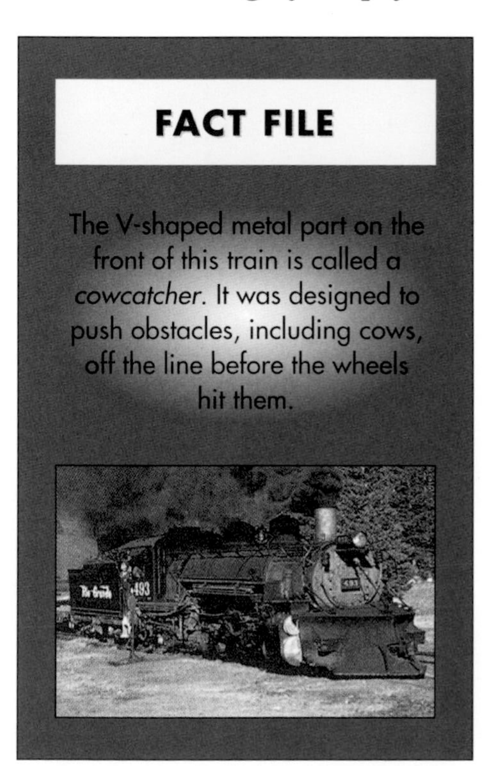

WHERE DID THE SALT MARCH TAKE PLACE?

Mohandas Gandhi (1869 to 1948), known as Mahatma Gandhi, was the father of the Indian nation. He helped free India from British control by a unique method of nonviolent resistance. He is still revered as one of the foremost spiritual and political leaders of the twentieth century.

Gandhi believed that nonviolence was a more effective way to get his message heard than violence, and in 1930, he protested against the British government's monopoly on salt. Possessing salt not bought from the government was a criminal offence. Gandhi protested this by leading his followers on a 240-mile march to the coast, where they made salt from seawater. Gandhi spent seven years in prison because of his protests against British injustice. He lived to see independence in 1947.

WHERE WAS THE BATTLE OF DIEN BIEN PHU?

Vietnam is a tropical country in southeast Asia. China governed the area from about 100 B.C. until 900 A.D., when the Vietnamese established an independent state. Fighting broke out between French forces and the Vietminh in 1946. It ended in 1954 with the French defeat in the Battle of Dien Bien Phu. An international conference to arrange a peace settlement also took place at this time. In 1957, Vietminh members in the South began to rebel against the South Vietnamese government. Fighting broke out, and it developed into the Vietnam War. The United States became the ally of the South.

FACT FILE

The Vietnam War lasted almost twenty years, starting in 1957 and ending in 1975. It was the longest war the U.S. was ever involved in.

WHY?

Contents

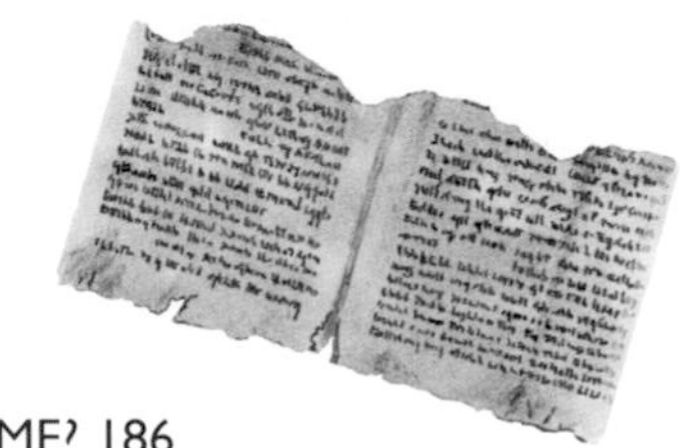

WHY DO THE ABORIGINES BELIEVE IN DREAM TIME?

FACT FILE

The Aborigines used ritual boomerangs, decorated with secret symbols, in magical dances. They were also used for hunting and for war.

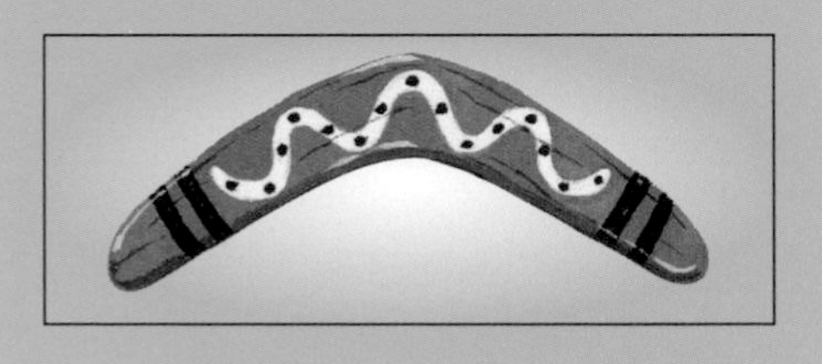

The Aborigines lived by gathering food and by hunting. Along the coast, they fished with nets, basket traps, and spears. In the bush, they used fire to drive animals into traps and made poisons from leaves and roots to drug fish in pools. Aborigines wore no clothing and rubbed animal fats onto their bodies to protect themselves from the cold.

Aboriginal rock artists looked "beneath the skin" to show a person's bones or organs. Paintings of people and animals are found at sites linked to the Aboriginal belief of the "Dream Time." This is the time when the spirits were supposed to have created the world.

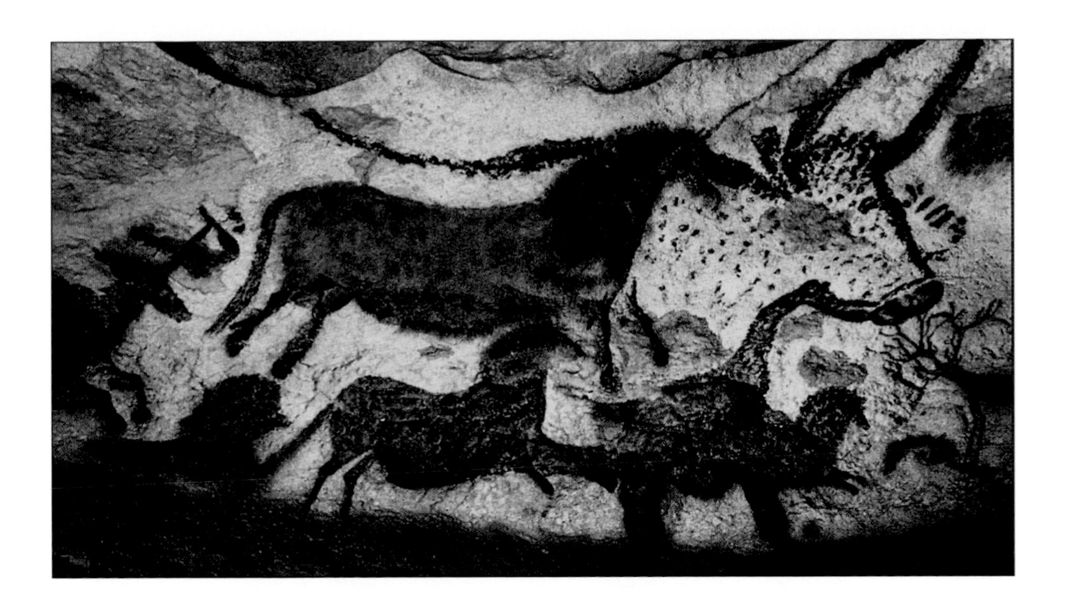

WHY DID CAVE PAINTERS PAINT?

Many thousands of years ago, people painted pictures of bulls, horses, and antelopes on the walls of their caves. We will never be sure why they actually did this. Perhaps, it was to make magic and bring people luck in their hunting. Another theory says that it might have been part of their religion. Cave artists used natural paints, which were made from colored earth and plant extracts. These paintings have been hidden from view for thousands of years. Viewed by the flickering light of burning torches, as they would have been viewed when first painted, the animals almost seem to come to life.

FACT FILE

Wooly mammoths were found painted on the walls of caves. As well as being an important source of meat, wooly mammoths provided skins for clothing and shelter. Their tusks were also carved into tools and ornaments.

WHY WERE LONGSHIPS CRUCIAL TO VIKING RAIDS?

A Viking longship

At a time when sailors dared not venture far from the coast, the Vikings boldly sailed out far across the Atlantic in their small, open longships. The Viking longships were fast and very strong. They had a long slender hull with a single mast and sail. Vikings were very adept at crossing the oceans.

During the eighth century, the Vikings began to leave their homes in Scandinavia and to explore Europe in search of treasure and places to settle. The Viking invaders are remembered as ruthless raiders, and their routes took them throughout Europe.

FACT FILE

Both Viking men and women dressed in durable clothing made from linen or wool cloth. They wore shoes made from leather.

WHY DO ISLAMIC BELIEVERS FOLLOW THE KORAN?

The Koran is the holy book of the Islamic religion. It contains the words of Allah as revealed to Mohammed by the archangel Gabriel in a series of visions. The Koran is a series of verses, describing the ways in which Muslims should conduct their lives. It specifies daily prayers and emphasizes the need for brotherly love and charity between Muslims. Although Muslims do not worship Mohammed, they show him the greatest respect. They believe that the Koran is the word of Allah and was not composed by Mohammed.

FACT FILE

Mecca is the sacred city of the Islamic world. The city is closed to all nonbelievers. Each year, millions of Muslims visit in a pilgrimage.

The holy Koran

WHY IS THE SPHINX A MYSTERY?

FACT FILE

The sun god Ra was often portrayed as a sun disk. He appeared in other forms too, including a cat, a bird, and a lion.

Religion played an important part in Egyptian life. The Egyptians believed in many gods and goddesses. Gods looked after every aspect of life. Every town and city had its own god. Temples were dedicated to a particular god or a dead pharaoh. Pyramids are the oldest stone structures in the world. They were built as tombs to keep the body of the dead king safe for eternity, and perhaps, to ease his passage to the heavens. The Great Sphinx is a mysterious rock sculpture with a human head and the body of a lion. This was built near the pyramids, outside modern Cairo, but the exact reason why is unknown. Historians believe the Sphinx is older than the pyramids themselves.

The Great Sphinx

WHY DID THE EGYPTIANS PRACTICE MUMMIFICATION?

Tutankhamun

FACT FILE

Osiris, god of the dead, was often shown as a mummy on a throne, wearing the crown of Upper Egypt.

The Egyptians believed in an afterlife, to which human beings' souls traveled after death. They thought it was important that the bodies of the dead be preserved for life in the next world, and so, they developed techniques for mummification.

During mummification, a dead person's organs were removed, and the body was embalmed and dried, using salts and chemicals. Then, it was wrapped in linen bandages. It was placed inside a coffin. Even animals, such as cats and monkeys, were sometimes mummified. Thousands of mummies must have been made, but only about 1,000 survive today.

Tutankhamun (pictured above) became king of Egypt at the age of nine and died when he was about 18 years old. His tomb is one of more than 60 royal tombs that surround the Valley of the Kings. Its four rooms contained more than 5,000 objects, including ostrich feathers, model ships, a throne, and a gold death mask.

WHY DOES JERICHO HAVE A PLACE IN JEWISH HISTORY?

The Bible records that Abraham had two sons, Ishmael (the ancestor of the Arabs) and Isaac. Isaac had two sons, Esau and Jacob. Jacob (also called Israel) had twelve sons. These sons became the heads of the Twelve Tribes, the Israelites of the Bible.

The Israelites became wealthy and powerful people. Perhaps, they are remembered best for their conquering of the city of Jericho. At God's command, the walls of Jericho tumbled down at the sound of the Israelite army shouting and banging their drums.

FACT FILE

Solomon was the son of David, an Israelite king who ruled from 1010 to 970 B.C. David defeated the Philistines and enlarged the kingdom, making Jerusalem its capital city. Soloman was responsible for building the sacred Temple in Jerusalem.

WHY IS THE DOME OF THE ROCK CELEBRATED BY TWO RELIGIONS?

The Dome of the Rock, which stands in Jerusalem, is worshipped by both the Jews and the Muslims as a holy shrine. The Jews believe that the Dome of the Rock is built over the rock on which Abraham prepared to sacrifice his son Isaac to god. The Muslims believe that Muhammad rose to heaven from the very same rock.

FACT FILE

Moses, the leader of the Hebrew people, received the two tablets from God. The stone tablets bear the Ten Commandments, as described in the Old Testament. They became the basis for Jewish law.

WHY WAS THE ROMAN ARMY SO SUCCESSFUL?

The tortoise formation

The Roman army invented a method of warfare that persisted for 2,000 years. Its troops were rigorously trained and exercised and then divided into small detachments under the control of officers. Roman soldiers wore effective armor and developed tactics that allowed them to fight successfully against almost any enemy. The Roman army was particularly good at defense. They used closed ranks to protect themselves with large shields, which deflected arrows and spears. When they reached close quarters, they could use their own weapons. The group of soldiers shown above was called the *tortoise formation*. It proved to be successful against their Celtic enemies.

FACT FILE

Emperor Trajan built a monument to the Roman army that was about 100 feet high. This section shows Roman legionaires, who were builders as well as fighters, constructing a fort.

WHY DID THE ROMANS BREAK DOWN THEIR EMPIRE?

FACT FILE

Hadrian's Wall was built from the east to the west coast in an attempt to keep the northern tribes out of the occupied areas.

It soon became evident that the Roman Empire was too big to survive in its original form. A huge civil service and army were needed to maintain the empire, and these became extremely expensive. Also, there were numerous rebellions in different parts of the empire, mostly headed by army commanders with ambitions to become emperor. Eventually, in 284 A.D., Emperor Diocletian broke the Roman Empire into smaller self-governing units, each with its own army. The whole empire was split into two sections, eastern and western. Eventually, the Roman Empire weakened to such an extent that it was successfully attacked and overrun by invading barbarians.

The Sermon on the Mount

WHY DID THE ROMANS PERSECUTE CHRISTIANS?

The teachings of Jesus were spread widely by His followers after His death. At first, the Christians were ignored by the Romans, especially as they did not join in the Jewish rebellion against Roman rule in 66 A.D. However, the early Christians began to travel around the Roman Empire. When they reached Rome, they began to recruit new followers. The Roman authorities became concerned that this new religion would threaten the established order. The Romans did not object to the new religion itself, but they did object to the fact that it denied the emperor's divinity. The new religion appealed to the poor and to slaves, and its popularity was seen as a threat to Roman society. So, Romans began to persecute the Christians.

FACT FILE

The symbol of a fish was used by the early Christians in Rome as a secret symbol to identify themselves to other Christians. The symbol was simple and quick to draw. It was not likely to be noticed by the Romans.

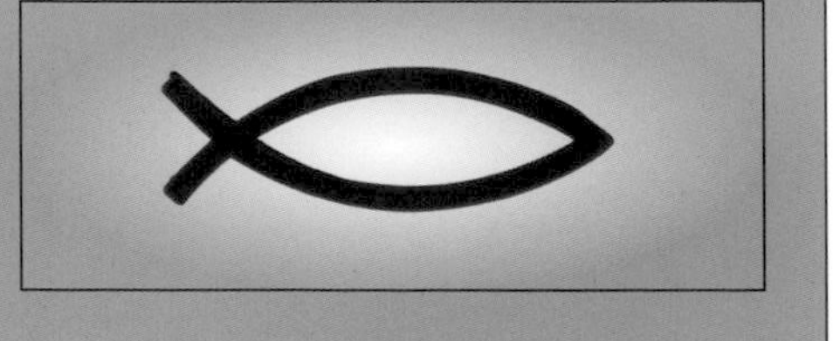

WHY WERE THE DEAD SEA SCROLLS HIDDEN?

The Dead Sea Scrolls are religious writings that were first discovered in 1947, hidden in caves near the Dead Sea. The dry atmosphere of the caves preserved the scrolls. About 800 scrolls have been found, mostly in a place called *Qumran* in Israel. They date from between 150 B.C. and 68 A.D., and they include all of the books of the Old Testament, or Hebrew Bible, except for Esther.

Scholars believe that the scrolls were concealed by members of a religious sect called the *Essenes*, who lived in this isolated community. They hid the scrolls to keep them safe during political unrest. They remained hidden for hundreds of years.

The museum in Jerusalem that holds the Dead Sea Scrolls

FACT FILE

The Dead Sea Scrolls are ancient documents written on leather and copper.

WHY WAS ATTILA THE HUN FEARED?

Attila the Hun

Attila was the ruler of the Hun kingdom, which is located in what is now called Hungary. The Huns began to expand beyond this area. They conquered surrounding countries until they controlled a region from the Rhine River to the Caspian Sea, extending all the way to the Baltic. The Huns were among the fiercest of the many barbarian tribes. They eventually destroyed the power of the Roman Empire. Attila, who is still renowned for his cruelty and the ferocity of his troops, led the Huns from their homeland. Together, they almost conquered Europe. He forced the Eastern Roman Empire to pay him a fee in exchange for not attacking them. He also demanded to marry the sister of the emperor of the Western Empire, with half the empire as a dowry. This request was refused and caused much bloodshed.

FACT FILE

A Roman coin stamped with the head of the Emperor Hadrian. During his reign, he personally visited nearly every province in the Roman Empire.

WHY DID THE FAMINE IN IRELAND BEGIN?

At the beginning of the 1800s, the population of Ireland stood at about 5,000,000 people. In the first 40 years of the century, the population increased to about 8,000,000. Many people lived in extreme poverty. In 1845, a fungus affected the vital potato crop in southern England. It soon spread to Ireland. With the failure of the potato crop, people began to die in thousands, either from hunger or disease.

The famine came to an end after 1849, when the potato crop only partially failed. By then, the population of Ireland had been reduced to just over 6,000,000 by famine and emigration.

FACT FILE

When Ireland's potato crop failed, people dug up their crops only to find them rotting in the ground.

DEPARTURE OF THE "NIMROD" AND "ATHLONE" STEAMERS, WITH EMIGRANTS ON BOARD, FOR LIVERPOOL.

FACT FILE

Japanese soldiers used iron swords and wore heavy armor. The bands of soldiers who served the land-owning lords became known as Samurai, the "knights" of medieval Japan.

WHY WAS FUJIWARA JAPAN A STRONG EMPIRE?

Prince Shotoku ruled Japan from 593 to 622 A.D., strongly encouraged by Chinese ways. Shotoku believed that the Japanese emperor should be all-powerful, like the ruler of China. In 858 A.D., however, the emperor lost control to a strong noble family called the *Fujiwaras*. The Fujiwaras had built up their power in the countryside, where they owned huge estates. Other nobles had also built up small empires of their own.

The Fujiwaras gradually won control of the emperors and of government by marrying their daughters into the imperial family. The Fujiwaras held onto power in Japan for 300 years. During this time, the great estates grew bigger and stronger, until the lords ruling them were almost like kings.

The Courting of the Fujiwaras

FACT FILE

Below, a paper-maker is at work, spreading wet pulp over a mesh frame. The invention of paper was announced by the director of the Chinese imperial workshops in 150 A.D. The Chinese began to use paper money under Sung rule.

WHY DID ANCIENT CHINA HAVE SUCH AN ADVANCED CIVILIZATION?

Chinese cities were a wonder to foreign visitors. Chang'an had more than one million citizens, yet its cleanliness was startling. There were public baths, and hot water was sold in the streets for washing. Toilet facilities in houses were fairly basic, emptying into cesspits, but waste was collected in carts every evening and taken away. The Chinese habit of using toilet paper came as another surprise to visitors.

The Chinese were fascinated by machines. They invented the wheelbarrow for carrying loads and even fitted barrows with sails to make pushing easier. They used waterwheels to mill rice and drive hammers to beat metal into shape. They knew about the magnetic compass, and their ships had stern rudders. Chinese soldiers had the best crossbows in the world and smoke and fire weapons.

WHY WAS THE TURKISH LEADER OSMAN SUCCESSFUL?

In about 1300, a Turkish leader called *Osman* ruled a small kingdom in Anatolia (modern Turkey). His family name in Arabic was Othman but is better known to us today as Ottoman.

Osman and his descendants were to build up one of the most important and long-lasting empires in world history. The Ottoman Turks started to take over parts of the weak Byzantine Empire. The new empire was a strong Muslim answer to the power of Christian Europe in the west.

In 1346, a Byzantine leader hired Ottomon troops to fight for him, but this turned out to be a big mistake. It allowed the Ottomans to cross into Europe, therefore increasing their empire.

FACT FILE

An intricately carved doorway marks the entrance to an Ottoman mosque.

WHY WAS TIMUR LANG NOTORIOUS?

FACT FILE

When Timur seized the city of Isfahan in 1387, he ordered his men to execute all 7,000 citizens and to pile their heads in huge mounds outside the city walls.

Timur Lang (or Timur the Lame) claimed to be a descendant of Genghis Khan and was a ruthless leader. When the Ottomans tried to expand their empire eastward, there was a shock in store for them. Timur had already conquered Persia and ravaged much of central Asia, including Russia and India, before the Ottomans attacked.

Timur fell on the Turks like a hurricane, ransacking their chief city in Anatolia, wiping out their army, and capturing their leader. Then, he began to loot their empire and break it up. That might have been the end of the Ottoman story, but in 1405, Timur died and the last of the Mongol kingdoms fell apart.

WHY WAS THE GREAT WALL OF CHINA BUILT?

The Great Wall of China is the longest structure ever built. Its total length, including older ruins, is about 3,977 miles. It was built with only basic tools. The wall crosses northern China between the east coast and north-central China.

Most of what is now called the *Great Wall* dates from the Ming dynasty (1368–1644). Under threat of Mongol invasion, the Ming government began to build the wall in the late fifteenth century, and this is what tourists see today. Like earlier ones, the wall protected China from minor attacks but proved no defense against major invasions.

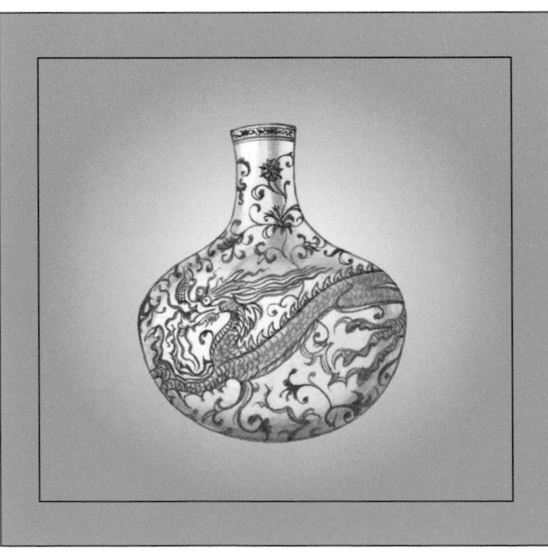

FACT FILE

Ming means *bright* in Chinese, and this period was important especially to the arts. Under the Ming emperors, art and literature flourished in China, notably the making of the blue and white pottery still famous today as Ming porcelain.

WHY WERE GUILDS FORMED?

A medieval shop

FACT FILE

Each occupation, including these blacksmiths, had its own guild. The guilds fixed prices and standards of work and made sure that their members were well paid.

The late Middle Ages saw a return to the idea of living in cities. After the merchants and craftsmen settled into towns, they set up organizations called *guilds*. A guild protected its members against unfair business practices, established prices and wages, and settled disputes between workers and employers.

Guilds played an important part in town government. When the first guilds were organized, the towns had few laws to protect their merchants. Most laws were made and enforced by the lord, who owned the land on which a town stood. As the townspeople gained power, they demanded the right to govern themselves. All workers in a guild trade had to go through a long and hard training process. The guilds soon grew rich and powerful as they were able to set the prices that all the tradesmen in the guild were allowed to charge.

St. Peter's Church in Rome

WHY DID THE RENAISSANCE TAKE PLACE?

The Renaissance began in Italy. Rome, the capital city, had been one of the main centers of the classical world. It was full of magnificent old buildings and other objects that inspired the "rebirth" of culture.

Money was an important reason why the Renaissance started in Italy. The Italian city-states were home to many wealthy families, who were eager to pay for new paintings, sculptures, and architecture. Many of the great artists, who were available to do this work, lived in Italy. They made this one of the most stunningly creative periods in history.

FACT FILE

Below is a column designed by Andrea Palladio, one of the great Renaissance architects. His buildings were designed using classical ideas.

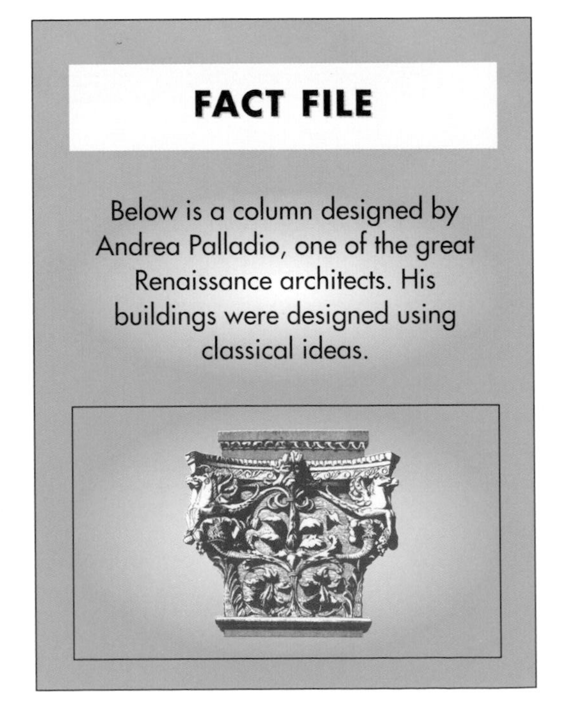

Head of Leda by Leonardo da Vinci

FACT FILE

Below are figures adorning the magnificent doors of the Baptistery, an eight-sided building on one of Florence's main piazzas.

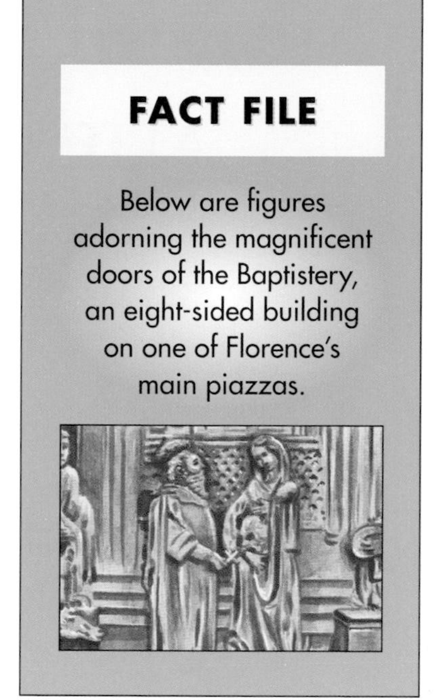

WHY WERE SO MANY ARTISTS LIBERATED DURING THE RENAISSANCE ERA?

For the first time since the classical period, artists felt free to show the beauty of the human body. They were encouraged by two things–the old Greek ideas of proportion and perspective, and the new research on how the body worked. A nude sculpture, such as Michelangelo's *David*, shows a deep knowledge of the action of muscles, sinews, and bones. Although all medieval art depicted religious subjects, Renaissance artists began to paint other things, such as landscapes and scenes of gods and goddesses from mythology. They also painted portraits of their patrons and of themselves, which expressed human beings' emotions more openly than ever before.

Lorenzo de Medici

WHY WERE DA VINCI'S IDEAS AHEAD OF HIS TIME?

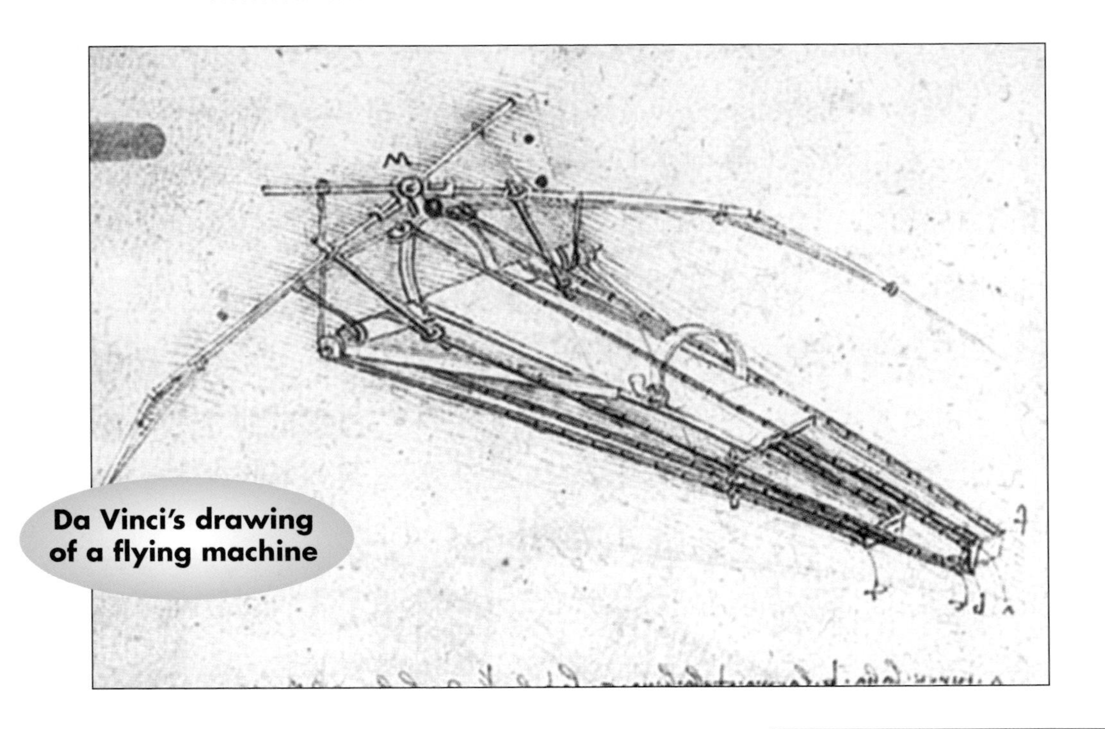

Da Vinci's drawing of a flying machine

During the Renaissance period, scientists and inventors were making important discoveries. They were asking questions which would change our view of the earth and the heavens forever. Of course, not all the inventions actually worked. The great artist and engineer Leonardo da Vinci was determined to find a way to make people fly like birds.

Throughout his life, Leonardo da Vinci drew many designs for flying machines. Among these were a kind of parachute and a helicopter with spinning blades. His grandest idea was for an aircraft with flapping wings, which he designed in 1503. He organized a test flight, but according to legend, the machine crashed. The first successful aircraft did not actually fly for another 400 years. So, DaVinci was certainly ahead of his time.

FACT FILE

Galileo Galilei was both an astronomer and a physicist. His observations about the heavens helped to confirm the ideas of Copernicus.

WHY IS COPERNICUS REMEMBERED?

FACT FILE

Galileo's telescopes were more powerful than any that had been used before. He was the first person to study the night sky through a telescope.

Nicolaus Copernicus was a Polish astronomer. Pictured below is his view of the Universe. He proposed that it was the sun not the earth that was at the center of the universe. The earth and the other planets simply revolved around it.

His idea was proved accurate in the 1620s when the Italian Galileo Galilei used an early telescope to observe the planet Jupiter. He could clearly see that there were other moons in orbit around Jupiter. Here were bodies which were not moving round the earth. This meant that the earth was not the center of the universe.

Luther at Wittenberg Castle

WHY DID THE REFORMATION TAKE PLACE?

Martin Luther was a Catholic monk from Germany. In 1510, he visited Rome, the home of the Catholic church, and was deeply shocked. He saw the Pope and his household living in great luxury and realized that the church was saturated with wealth and power. Luther nailed his list of 95 arguments against the church's sale of indulgences to the door of Wittenberg Castle in 1517. His ideas quickly spread across northern Europe. He begged the nobles of Germany to help him reform the old religion. This alarmed the Pope, who sent an order declaring that Luther was a heretic.

FACT FILE

During the Reformation, the Bible became available for all to read, thanks to new printing technology. Also, for the first time, it was translated from Latin into local languages.

WHY DID KING HENRY VIII DEFY THE POPE?

Henry VIII

As Martin Luther's ideas spread, reformers, known as *Protestants*, emerged throughout Europe. A theological debate followed that eventually erupted into religious warfare. It lasted for well over a century.

In England, Henry VIII initially defended the Catholic church. However, the lengths to which Henry VIII went to get a male heir shocked Europe. In 1509, he married Catherine of Aragon, but when all her sons died in infancy, Henry wanted the marriage declared invalid. The Pope refused this request. As a consequence, Henry cut all ties between England and the Catholic Church in Rome. He declared himself Supreme Head of the Church of England.

FACT FILE

Excommunicated by the Pope, Henry gave himself unrestricted power and set about consolidating the spiritual independence of England from Rome. In 1536, Henry VIII ordered that monasteries such as Tintern Abbey be dissolved, closed down, or ransacked.

WHY DID THE SPANISH ARMADA SET OUT TO ATTACK?

Philip of Spain had once hoped to return England to Catholicism by marrying Queen Elizabeth. She refused him, so he decided to change England's religion by force. In 1588, Philip assembled a fleet of 130 ships and sent them to pick up soldiers from the Netherlands and invade England. The great Spanish Armada sailed across the English Channel but never reached its goal. The remnants of the Armada struggled into Spanish seaports during autumn of 1588.

The defeat of the Armada did not end the war with Spain. It dragged on for another sixteen years.

FACT FILE

Mary Queen of Scots was not a good ruler. In 1568, she was forced to flee Scotland and find refuge in England, throwing herself on the mercy of Elizabeth I.

WHY WAS THE REIGN OF ELIZABETH I SUCCESSFUL?

Despite a traumatic early life–her mother was executed when she was only three and her half-sister Mary had her imprisoned during her brief reign–Elizabeth displayed strength and prudence as Queen. Strong-willed like her father Henry VIII, Elizabeth I was fair and grateful to devoted servants, picking advisers who proved able and loyal. In 1559, she pushed through laws which confirmed England as a Protestant nation. Priests were ordered to use the new English Prayer Book. Elizabeth ended her reign as one of the best-loved and most successful of all English rulers. Her country was stronger and more peaceful than it had ever been before.

FACT FILE

Elizabeth's signature on the death warrant of Mary Stuart. Elizabeth hesitated for days before signing it. She knew that Mary's death would give her Catholic enemies an excuse to attack her.

WHY DID A FARMING REVOLUTION TAKE PLACE?

In 1700, more than 90 percent of Europe's population lived in the countryside. Most were peasants working the land. They grew their own food, using tools and farming methods which had changed very little since medieval times. By 1800, the number of people in Europe soared from 120,000,000 to over 180,000,000. Farmers needed to find ways to grow much bigger quantities of crops so that there was enough food to feed many more people. So, the farming revolution took place.

FACT FILE

As a result of improved breeding techniques, farmers were able to produce sheep which gave better wool. They also had short legs and barrel-like bodies for more meat.

WHY WAS THE PRACTICE OF CROP ROTATION SUCCESSFUL?

The medieval system of growing crops was wasteful. By about 1650, Dutch farmers had developed a more efficient way of "rotating" their crops. Instead of leaving a field fallow, they made it fertile more quickly by spreading manure or growing clover and grasses to improve the soil.

In the 1730s, farmers, such as Charles Townshend of England, began using a four-part system of planting crops in rotation. In this system, wheat was grown in the first year and turnips in the second. Sheep or cattle ate the turnips, providing valuable manure. Barley was sown in the third year, then grass or clover. This method was widely adopted and became known as the "four-course crop rotation system."

Four-course crop rotation

FACT FILE

Since farming began, farmers had scattered seed by hand. Jethro Tull's seed drill put the seed directly into the soil in neat rows.

WHY DID GARIBALDI UNIFY ITALY?

The Treaty of Paris that brought the Crimean War to an end did little to bring stability to Europe. The leader of Sardinia-Piedmont, Count Cavour, used the meetings at Paris to demand unification in Italy. At that time, Italy was made up of many separate states, most controlled by Austria. The movement for independence, known as the *Risorgimento*, started in the 1820s and 1830s. In 1858, Sardinia-Piedmont allied itself with France and drove out the Austrians from much of northern Italy. The successful revolt by Guiseppe Garibaldi and his "red shirts" led eventually to the unification of all of Italy. Italy was declared a kingdom under King Victor-Emmanuel II in 1861. Rome was captured and made the capital of a unified Italy in 1871.

FACT FILE

In 1848, people in Paris took to the streets to demand a new republic, as well as votes for all males. Government soldiers shot and killed some of the rioters.

WHY WERE DAVY LAMPS USED?

During the time of the Industrial Revolution, coal became increasingly important as the fuel for ovens and forges. Coal mines were dug deeper into the earth as demand grew, leading to greater dangers of flood, collapse, and gas explosions. Inventions, such as Newcomen's steam pump to remove water and Davy's safety lamp, eased these problems.

Davy's safety lamp warned miners of gas leaks underground. Inventions such as this only encouraged coal miners to dig to farther and more dangerous depths.

Abraham Darby's discovery that coal could be turned into coke led to the production of coke-smelted iron. The improved iron could be used to make everything from ploughs and bridges to steam engines and drilling machines.

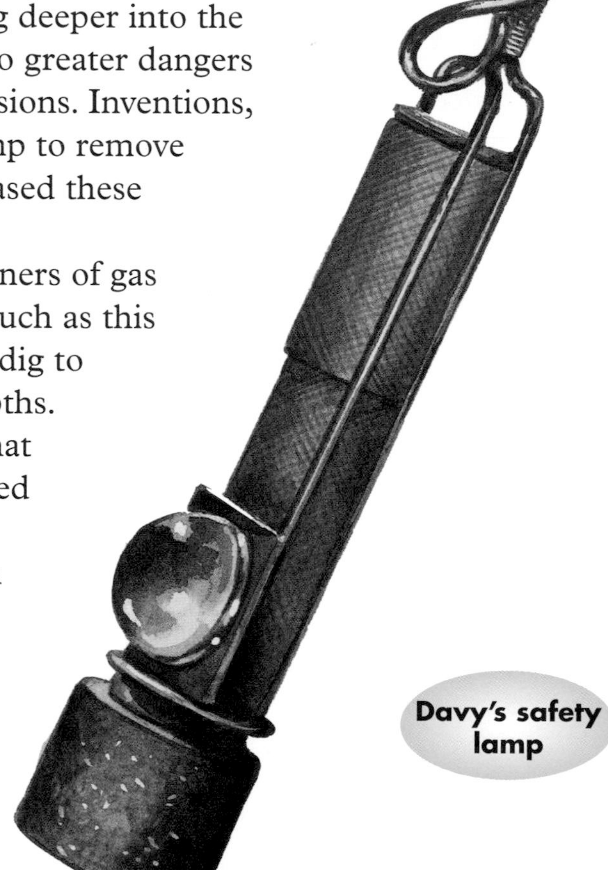

Davy's safety lamp

FACT FILE

Benjamin Franklin was an American statesman as well as a scientist. Franklin proved that lightning and electricity are the same thing by flying a kite in a storm. He was struck by lightning but survived.

WHY DID THE U.S.A. ENTER WORLD WAR I?

From the start of World War I, British warships blockaded German seaports. In this way, Britain's navy prevented supplies from reaching Germany, causing severe shortages of food and other goods. The Germans retaliated with their submarines, called *U-boats*. After 1915, U-boats attacked both warships and merchant shipping carrying supplies to Britain. In May 1915, a German torpedo hit a British passenger ship called the *Lusitania*. The ship was carrying nearly 2,000 passengers, including many Americans. The sinking of the Lusitania was one of the factors that eventually drew the United States into the war.

FACT FILE

Poppies bloomed on many of the French battlefields of World War I. Today, artificial poppies are sold in America and in Europe to raise money for war veterans.

WHY IS FLORENCE NIGHTINGALE REMEMBERED?

Florence Nightingale was an English nurse who single-handedly revolutionized nursing practices, sanitation in hospitals, and public health in the nineteenth century. When war broke out in the Crimea, Nightingale volunteered for duty, leaving with 38 nurses in her charge. She organized the barracks hospital after the Battle of Inkerman, and by introducing discipline and hygiene to hospitals, she managed to reduce the death toll. When she returned to England in 1856, she was rewarded with about $35,000 for her work.

FACT FILE

Florence Nightingale was known as the "Lady with the Lamp" because of the light she carried at night. She would walk through the hospital halls, checking on her patients.

WHY DID THE FIRST SETTLERS ARRIVE IN AUSTRALIA?

Commemorative Australian stamps of Cook's arrival in Botany Bay

In April 1770, Captain James Cook had sailed along the east coast of Australia. He and his crew landed at a place called *Botany Bay* and claimed the land for Britain, naming the region New South Wales.

Eighteen years later, in 1788, the first ships full of settlers arrived from Britain. These settlers were all convicts, transported from Britain for various crimes. Under the command of Captain Arthur Philip, the convicts were set to work founding a penal colony in nearby Sydney. About 300,000 Aborigines were living in Australia when the settlers first arrived from Europe. They were divided into about 500 tribal groups.

FACT FILE

Convicts were transported to Australia and confined in prison ships like this one. By 1830, about 58,000 convicts were in Australia.

WHY WERE THE D-DAY LANDINGS A TURNING POINT IN THE WAR?

In June 1944, Allied leaders decided that it was time to attack Germany. Under the overall command of U.S. General Eisenhower, Allied troops landed in Normandy and advanced across France. Meanwhile, Soviet troops moved across eastern Europe.

On the morning of June 6, 1944, thousands of Allied troops went ashore along the coast of Normandy in northern France. These events became known as the *D-Day landings*.

FACT FILE

Charles de Gaulle was leader of the French troops, known as the *Free French*, who had escaped occupied France. After the war, he became one of France's most powerful presidents ever.

D-Day landings

WHY WAS ISRAEL CREATED?

At the end of World War II, the demands for a Jewish state in Palestine grew. In 1947, the United Nations took over responsibility for Palestine, dividing it into an Arab state and a Jewish state. The Jews agreed to this plan, but the Arabs did not. The state of Israel came into being on May 14, 1948. It was immediately attacked by Arab armies from Egypt, Syria, Lebanon, Iraq, and Transjordan (Jordan). These countries are known collectively as the Arab League. By 1949, Israel had defeated the Arab League and added land to its own territory.

FACT FILE

Civil war broke out between Christians and Muslims in Lebanon in 1975. Fighting caused extensive damage in Beirut.

WHY DID THE COLD WAR START?

After World War II, the United States and the USSR (Union of Soviet Socialist Republics) emerged as the two main powers in the world. They were known as *superpowers*. Although they had fought together to defeat Nazi Germany, differences between the two superpowers soon led to the start of the Cold War.

The Cold War was a political war between the USSR and its communist allies and the U.S.A. and other noncommunist countries. It did not involve fighting, although there was a threat of military action on several occasions.

FACT FILE

In 1945, the three Allied leaders–Winston Churchill, Franklin D. Roosevelt, and Joseph Stalin–met at Yalta to discuss the problems facing postwar Europe.

The Berlin airlift

PICTURE ACKNOWLEDGMENTS

Corbis U.K. Ltd. / Bettmann 61, / Charles & Josette Lenars 92